Successful Marriage

A FAMILY SYSTEMS APPROACH TO COUPLES THERAPY

Successful Marriage

A FAMILY SYSTEMS APPROACH TO COUPLES THERAPY

W. Robert Beavers, M.D.

Clinical Director, Southwest Family Institute;
Clinical Professor of Psychiatry,
University of Texas Health Science Center,
Dallas, Texas

W · W · NORTON & COMPANY
New York · London

Published simultaneously in Canada by Penguin Books Canada Ltd,
2801 John Street, Markham, Ontario L3R 1B4

Printed in the United States of America.

Library of Congress Cataloging in Publication Data

Beavers, W. Robert, 1929–
  Successful marriage.

  Bibliography: p.
  Includes index.
  1. Marital psychotherapy. I. Title.
RC488.5.B38 1985   616.89'156   84-27200

ISBN 0-393-70006-2

W. W. Norton & Company, Inc., 500 Fifth Avenue, New York, N.Y. 10110

W. W. Norton & Company Ltd., 37 Great Russell Street, London WC1B 3NU

  3 4 5 6 7 8 9 0

For Jeanette and for our children,
Bruce and Bonnie,
who now provide a different perspective
for us to learn about couples.

FOREWORD

Everyone knows that marriage is an impossible state. How can any two people, imprinted by their family of origin as to what is the "right" way of thinking and doing things, possibly relate to each other with any degree of compatibility? Whitaker has wondered if marriage could be thought of as a form of mental illness, a kind of folie à deux, and he thinks that, on one level, marriage produces "hateful demons out of perfectly nice people." On the other hand, he believes it is a growthful experience and the only way to get a Ph.D. in interpersonal relationships. I myself have stated that marriage can be a therapeutic system or a degradation of the human spirit and that it provides the context for bottomless hatred and exultant intimacy, idyllic fusion and sweet, anachronistic revenge.

Aside from its alleged inherent absurdity, marriage is an incredibly intricate phenomenon, simultaneously existing on multiple levels, stretching back to the past, and built on incommunicable experiences. The behavioral sciences have only isolated a scattered few of the million or so variables of marriage. Bob Beavers, in this extraordinary book addressed to marital therapists, has added more crucial dimensions to the understanding of the mystery of marriage. As I read through the chapters I kept getting jolts of recognition of familiar things I have observed in couples I have treated. I particularly liked the way he integrated the case examples with the clinical principles, thus making the material come alive with real people. *Successful Marriage* contains the accumulated wisdom of a very experienced and remarkably human clinician who is aware of the traps, pitfalls and pleasures of treating marital distress. He and I both agree that the best way to help children is to help the relationship between the parents, whether married, separated or divorced. Bob gives hope that marriage relationships do not have to be crazy as they sometimes are.

The book is primarily aimed at enabling helpers to, as Bob puts it, "get their heads straight." Here is a sample of Beavers' clinically useful and wise messages to marital therapists:

- "To thine own self be true." (This Shakespearean aphorism expresses the dictum that a therapist's first obligation is to himself or herself.)
- It is necessary to deal with symptoms at various system levels. (The individual as a system has been lost by some family therapists, who only want to deal with sequences of interaction.)
- Clients need to be held responsible for their behavior. (The greatest gift we can give clients is the sense that they are ultimately responsible for their own experiences.)
- Emotional illness is a "deficiency of satisfying, coherent, self-defining experiences with meaningful others." (It is noteworthy that Beavers defines emotional illness in interpersonal terms. His precept is consonant with Fairbairn's fundamental postulate that the basic human motive is to strive toward a satisfying relationship.)
- A systems approach is more likely to be successful in couples treatment. (From a systems viewpoint there are no villains in families, and there are no bad or sick individuals in a disturbed marriage. The existing research comparing systems marital therapy with traditional individual therapy for marital problems shows the clear superiority of the systems approach.)

- Couples therapy can be as effective in altering character problems as individual therapy. (This statement should surprise a lot of therapists, but I believe it to be true.)
- It is necessary to identify the ''spin-outs'' in couple therapy—that is, those shared, stereotyped, repetitive, and predictable sequences of behavior of couples in therapy. (All marital therapists have at times despaired of tracking or interrupting these rigid patterns. As the poet once said, ''Christ, what are patterns for?'')
- Internal conflicts are transmuted into marital blame. (This process is central to my own thesis of the interpersonal resolution of intrapsychic conflict. Married people do indeed project split-off, disowned aspects of the self onto the partners, and then fight these traits in the partner. In this connection I wish Beavers had cited the towering work of Henry Dicks of Tavistock.)
- Grown people assume the child's position in marital disharmony, and make a fearsome authority figure out of the spouse and therapist. (To me this phenomenon demonstrates the power of the family of origin that operates in all of us, which is why I routinely bring in the family of origin of each spouse.)
- Why is it that people, who have great social skills in the outside world, lose these skills in dealing with their partner? (We give to our intimates the best and worst that is in us. Toward these people we will manifest our greatest cruelty, but for them we will make our greatest sacrifices.)

In Ingmar Bergman's play ''Scenes from a Marriage'' the wife says of a couple she knows, ''They don't speak the same language. They must translate into a third language they both understand in order to get each other's meaning.'' When he treats a couple Beavers offers them a third language which translates the private meanings of each partner into a transactional language which crosses the gulf of misunderstanding.

We are privileged to be allowed into Beavers' treatment room and share in the struggles of couples and Bob's sensitive and skillful efforts to reduce their pain and help them develop a mutually satisfying relationship. Bob Beavers has made a major contribution by extending his pioneering work with normal families into successful marriages.

James L. Framo, Ph.D.
San Diego, California
January, 1985

CONTENTS

Section Three
CHRONIC MARITAL CONFLICT

PREFACE

This book is a statement of where I am now in understanding people's problems and possibilities. I was trained as a wet lab scientist and left medical school basic science research 25 years ago to become a psychiatrist, thinking I would bring biochemical enlightenment to the dark corners of the field. Instead, I was captured by the power of family interactional patterns in making or breaking human lives.

My first patient as a psychiatric resident taught me a principle that underlies all of my work with troubled people. A shy, awkward 17-year-old from a poor family, Nancy impulsively married an AWOL soldier, became pregnant and then became acutely psychotic following the birth of her child. She was in the psychiatric unit with a roommate, "Mrs. Meany," a middle-income married woman with a history of intimidating, hostile behavior, including tantrums in which she destroyed objects in her vicinity. Nancy loved pretty things, and her prized possession in an otherwise barren room was a green potted plant on which she lavished tender care. One day she came to my office, pale, shaken, and barely able to speak. Slowly, hesitantly, she described a violent outburst by her roommate that had culminated in the destruction of Nancy's plant. I asked her what she had done about it and she said, "Oh, nothing—after all, *she's sick.*"

In our subsequent exploration of this event, Nancy and I came to see that if she were able to confront Mrs. Meany and successfully negotiate what she wanted, she would have a new plant and her roommate would be, by being held accountable for her acts, a step further toward being a responsible person. Nancy had believed that her advantage would be at the expense of her roommate's "health." We recognized, as we worked together, that either both would win or both would lose. A simple insight, perhaps, but one that is missing with most people in emotional pain, who view relationships as battles and their own desires, hungers, and longings as threatening, not only to others close to them but also to society at large.

My subsequent experiences in psychiatry have amplified and underscored this principle. Win/lose battles produce only victims and no victors. When people are considered valuable and worthy of respect, each one's needs intertwine and complement those of the other. Such an underpinning of belief, based on increasing clinical observation and research, encourages—even demands—an approach to individual emotional problems that includes working with an identified patient, but also with spouses, parents, children, and whole families in order to help them develop needed living skills.

In the subsequent years of active practice, I have pursued the elusive goals of integrating biological, individual, dyadic, family, and social factors in alleviating human pain and dysfunction. Curiosity about family patterns led to studies of healthy families, and this has remained a strong emphasis—finding the strengths and coping abilities in people, reinforcing and broadening them.

Research and clinical work have always been inseparable for me; I must enrich one with the other. Past and present family research is the backbone of this book on couples.

ACKNOWLEDGMENTS

I owe the existence of this book to the kindness and caring of many: my patients, who have instructed me, negotiated with me, and at important times been tolerant; Jeanette, my wife, who has worked hard and sensitively in editing the manuscript; and Diane Rotolo, my secretary, who is all alertness and patience.

Chapter 1, "Indications and Contraindications," is a highly modified version of a paper I wrote with the same title for *Psychiatric Clinics of North America*, Vol. 5, No. 3, pp. 469–478, December 1982.

Chapter 3, "Attributes of the Healthy Couple," is a modified version of a chapter with the same title written for R. Stahmann and W. Hiebert, *Counseling in Marital and Sexual Problems: A Clinician's Handbook*, 3rd Edition, D. C. Heath & Co., 1984.

Chapter 8, "Approaching Families of Origin From a Systems Perspective," is a later version of a chapter written for H. Liddle, *Clinical Implications of the Family Life Cycle*, Aspen Publications, 1983.

"Lessons From a Dancing Chicken" in Chapter 9 was written for my column in the AAMFT newspaper.

Successful Marriage

A FAMILY SYSTEMS APPROACH TO COUPLES THERAPY

INTRODUCTION

This is an idea book, not specifically a how-to book. The distinction is important as it reflects both my teaching style and my beliefs about being helpful to people. Students, like patients, come looking for techniques that will make them successful. Their aim is neither surprising nor reprehensible, but it is doomed to disappointment. There is, I believe, no shortcut or magic formula, inasmuch as the basic requirement of the competent therapist is to become *a self-aware human being who has values and standards, who understands the differences between style and substance, and who has both.*

Parents, overwhelmed by the complexities of their own survival and well-being, as well as by responsibility for their children, often desire a "quick fix," directives to solve relationship problems stemming from lack of education, lack of modeling, or lack of practice. Their search is usually futile. In recent years a program called Parent Effectiveness Training has attempted to define and teach successful parenting techniques encompassing systems concepts of boundaries, circularity of cause and effect, etc. Unfortunately, outcome studies have found no demonstrable lasting benefit for parents who have undergone the training program (30).

This is consistent with my clinical experience. Years ago I had an opportunity to treat some psychiatric residents and their spouses at the same time the residents were undergoing an "empathy training" course. Sadly, there seemed to

3

be no payoff in their own family relationships resulting from the empathy training.

I have arrived at the position that if helpers (whether parents or teachers or psychotherapists) ''have their heads straight,'' that is, are clear regarding their basic beliefs and understanding of human systems, their responses will generally be effective and useful. However, if these persons are confused, unintegrated (lacking integrity), or looking to others as absolute authorities, almost any intervention they try will be inadequate. So, my teaching and this book are attempts to enable helpers to get their heads straight. Toward this end I hope to present as clearly as possible my beliefs, their sources (research, clinical work, personal experience), references to these sources, and a continual awareness of stylistic differences that are, I believe, important to the particular therapist but not correlated with good results.

This approach is also consistent with research into healthy families, whose similar family processes may appear with very different family styles. Useful and effective psychotherapists likewise induce similar processes by using many different styles and techniques.

I hope the readers of this text on treating couples will be strengthened and broadened in their knowledge and beliefs, will develop a greater skepticism about the universal value of specific interventions, and will, with increasing freedom and confidence, claim various possible interventions as their own while defining others as foreign to their sense of self.

In the past quarter century, a broadened definition of emotional illness has evolved. The broader conceptual framework of a systems approach (5) considers illness or health to be a function of many levels of human systems—from neurotransmitter substances through neural organization, individual temperament and character, dyadic patterns, family organizations, and social structure (8). Each level influences the other, and human health cannot be well understood or treated without awareness of multiple levels.

Systems
holism "

This approach is a large "umbrella," comprehensively integrating the various data of mental and emotional illness. My goal is to present a systems framework for couples therapy that can be integrated with, for example, a neurotransmitter theory of depression. These seemingly disparate understandings of psychiatric illness are quite compatible when viewed from a multilevel systems orientation. Presaged by Harry Stack Sullivan's interpersonal theory of psychiatry (46), this trend is currently well identified by the term *systems*, as in "a systems view of emotional illness and health." Its profoundly different conceptual framework for understanding depression, psychosis, and behavioral problems offers, on the one hand, possibilities for more effective and humanistic treatment. On the other hand, if not properly understood, it can be misused to attack family members of severely emotionally ill people as responsible for the illness (3) and to blur the painful fact that we individual humans are responsible for our lives.

In order to embrace a systems perspective of emotional problems and still retain some control of the multiple variables involved in the development and amelioration of symptoms, psychotherapists have often limited this extension of focus to the family, though some brave (grandiose?; foolhardy?) souls have made forays outside that boundary to include other significant persons in the human network, from neighbors to the postman (43). Family therapy has become a powerful force in the mental health field, with great enthusiasm but only modest research, few follow-up studies, and no uniformity of training programs.

Psychopathology, according to this view, is not defined as something within one person, but includes interactional patterns; treatment consists of altering these patterns with the expected result of individual improvement. The definition of these patterns has been, in the main, a function of different therapists' preferences and their ideas of what the ideal pattern should be. Sensitive clinicians, charismatic performers, intense authoritarians, and gentle egalitarians have developed theories and practices based largely on their own personalities, and often these are altered little, if at all, by the nature of the identified patient or the particular family.

It was primarily for this reason that, after 10 years of research focusing on the relationship of family patterns and individual psychopathology in families with an adolescent schizophrenic (10, 11), I rejoiced at the opportunity to be the research consultant to a group planning to study interactional pattens in both healthy and disturbed families. This offered a means of developing a rich resource of family data with potential for providing structure and direction in the field of family therapy. After six years of work together, the Timberlawn group (Jerry M. Lewis, myself, John Gossett, and Virginia Phillips) reported its findings in a book, *No Single Thread* (36). The excitement and possiblities engendered by this research material led me to write of its implications for individual and group psychotherapy in *Psychotherapy and Growth: A Family Systems Perspective* (5) and also provided the emotional fuel and much of the background for this book. Several summary statements derived from the Timberlawn study can provide the reader with a mental set useful in work with couples as well as in reading this book. I will list them here and recommend that the diligent and curious consult the books mentioned above for more details.

1) There is high correlation between the degree of family competence, based on reliable rater judgments, and the degree of dysfunction of an adolescent psychiatric patient member of these families. Though many other variables are important in the evolution of patienthood, family competence as determined by interactional patterns is a powerful influence.
2) There are identifiable patterns of family interaction associated with various kinds of individual psychopathology

and with degrees of family competence. In addition, there are consistent contrasting family patterns found in healthy families that suggest possible directions for therapists in their attempts at useful intervention.

3) The quality of the parental coalition in intact families is highly correlated with overall family competence and with the capability of their children. Further, the observed coalition was closely related to the reported comfort and satisfaction of the partners.

Psychoanalytic theory, developmental theory, systems theory, learning theory, interactional research, and clinical observations are all part of a coherent guide to the etiology and strategies for treating emotional illness. In *Psychotherapy and Growth* these sources of information were capsuled in the definition of emotional illness that is also used here: *a deficiency of satisfying, coherent, self-defining experiences with meaningful others*. From this umbrella statement of origins, treatment naturally follows as the provision of such experiences by interaction with the therapist, the spouse, other family members, and the host of potentially available people that surround us in this increasingly crowded planet. Patients are helped to see others not as threats to their survival and integrity but as partners in living.

This book is about therapeutic intervention engineered by inviting the basic unit of a family—the couple—to work together with a trained psychotherapist. It will cover the important task of intervening in crisis, as well as the tough but satisfying job of ongoing intensive growth promotion.

Section One
GENERAL
CONSIDERATIONS

1 INDICATIONS AND CONTRAINDICATIONS

Couples therapy may be defined as a strategy of psychotherapeutic treatment that arranges to intervene in a committed couple's relationship. Such a couple may be of the same sex or heterosexual, formally married or living together; in any case, one or both have requested professional help.

The origins of this approach in psychiatry predate the development of a systems orientation; with emotional illness then assumed to be simply an individual phenomenon, one member of a couple would be defined by both partners and by the therapist as "ill," and the therapist would enlist the cooperation of the partner in treating him or her. Meanwhile, in the broader field of human relations, psychologists, social workers, and ministers were frequently asked to do "marriage counseling" with couples who viewed themselves as healthy but unhappy. Experiencing problems in the bittersweet coil of an ongoing commitment, these people sought help beyond that which might be available from family and friends, bartenders and hairdressers.

The relatively recent development of family therapy as a body of theory and practice has resulted in a more complex orientation to marital therapy. The "identified patient" is redefined as a marker signaling trouble in family attitudes and patterns. A psychotherapist can then select the family intervention strategy that seems most likely to effectively alter these patterns, seeing one person, the couple, the

11

whole family, or using several of these approaches sequentially. In other words, all psychotherapy can be viewed as family systems intervention, and the choice of which family members one sees is a most significant decision.

Any or all of these approaches (identified patient, counseling, and interactional patterns and processes) can be used with different couples or with the same couple at different times, depending on the problems they present. One of the advantages of a systems view is its inherent flexibility, linking intervention strategies to types of problems and thus freeing therapists (and patients) from "cookbook" methods. In most treatment settings, the psychoanalyst analyzes, the organically oriented physician dispenses electroconvulsive therapy or drugs, the family therapist convenes the family, the marriage counselor sees the couple. By contrast, the systems-oriented therapist can vary his approaches and can also recognize when to refer to other therapists for techniques in which he or she is unskilled.

It has been my clinical experience that couples therapy can be effective as crisis intervention and as relatively superficial "adjustment" assistance. It can also be a powerful tool, the primary instrument, in bringing about the recovery of a psychiatric patient. Further, if patients and therapist agree, the opportunities to alter character patterns and to produce individual growth are as great with a couples approach as with any other form of psychotherapy, including intensive individual treatment. The bonus with psychotherapy of the couple is, of course, the expectation that their dyadic and family patterns will change for the better.

WHEN COUPLES THERAPY IS INDICATED

The simplest indication for couples strategy results from the increasingly frequent request of a marital pair, neither of whom is psychotic or severely depressed, for such help.

Pressure for the request usually comes from one spouse, with the other reluctantly agreeing. Though both wish the relationship to continue, their dialogue in the first interview is usually tinged with despair.

Case Example. A 38-year-old research engineer phoned, asking that he and his wife, a 36-year-old graduate student in philosophy, be seen. They appeared together, he looking like a schoolboy in the principal's office, she vibrating with anxiety and poorly disguised resentment. They had two latency-age children, and she had been struggling diligently with the dual responsibilities of graduate work and homemaking. Having previously had a year of individual psychotherapy, she believed herself to be filled with emotional insight. She described her husband as preoccupied, passive, hopelessly inept in family responsibilities and also in lovemaking. He, in turn, admitted his passivity (whatever that meant to these people), but said that she attacked him so stubbornly and so repeatedly that he could only withdraw and go on with his work. He had accepted her definition of the problem as one that they shared, but this admission was less heartfelt than it was characteristic of his pattern of docile peacekeeping.

The wife was clearly more agitated and emotional and was closer to conscious despair. She was most wary of being designated as "sick" because of her history of having sought psychiatric help, and this spurred her to greater maneuvers to blame the husband.

The emerging picture was more complex than simply two people who wanted to relate better. Though both presented themselves as desiring to work together, each wanted the other to change. Their way of entering treatment illustrated their usual way of operating: He was defined as passive, though he made the appointment, while she was assumed to feel the most pain but expected him to do something.

There were, however, several factors that made couples intervention promising. Neither partner had an intensely invested outside romantic involvement. Each was able to carry on daily activities to the satisfaction of everyone except the spouse. They

cared about maintaining a family, and both were willing to explore
the possibilities of improving an unsatisfactory relationship.

A second indication for couples therapy is the existence
of a stalemate in individual psychotherapy because of the
tenacious projection of power, control, and responsibility
onto the absent spouse.

Patients in individual treatment uniformly use projection
as a defense. Projection, defined as externalizing some aspect of the intrinsic self, is a classic example of the short-
term advantage/long term disadvantage common to all maladaptive psychological mechanisms. Many frightened and
isolated people project unacceptable parts of themselves
onto the outside environment in socially bizarre ways that
draw attention to themselves as different or odd; for example, "The communists (or the FBI) are responsible for my
failures—they hound me and thwart every effort I make."
The disturbing quality of such eerie projections causes people to shy away from the speaker and define him as very
strange, even insane. But more commonly used projections
that are "homey" and ordinary sounding can be just as
damaging to any effort at personal growth. From Carla, a
22-year-old college graduate: "My mother keeps getting sick
and I have to quit my job." From Jean, a 50-year-old widow:
"I found the perfect man, but my children wouldn't let me
marry him." From John, a 35-year-old executive, "My wife
won't let me change jobs, but I tell you I will kill myself if
I have to continue dealing with this boss." What are the projections in these examples? Projections of the power to control and projections of the fear of change—such is the stuff
of dialogue between therapist and emotionally ill people.

An extremely frequent, "understandable" projection is
to the lover or spouse. The relationship in which a person
is most invested, most hopeful and most often disappointed
is the very place where skills in achieving intimacy are sorely

tried. "Understandable" is in quotes because relatively few friends, bartenders, or hairdressers see such projections as distancing or unacceptable, and they will usually support them. "My wife doesn't understand me." "Yeah, I know just what you mean." The social network effectively bolsters these projections and entraps the unhappy person in an ever tighter symbiosis with a spouse perceived as unrewarding.

The individual psychotherapist who attempts to challenge this reinforced projection often faces unacceptable alternatives. Developing an alliance with the spouse in treatment can passively encourage the projective defense, but vigorous challenges of the patient's perceptions can endanger necessary rapport. The frequency of both alternatives is all too evident in treatment situations and in families. Frustrating triangles are a natural result of the acceptance of projection, and these are often impetus for real or symbolic incestuous relationships between parents and children or for frustrating, poorly defined affairs, which are unwittingly set up as ideal for use in the battle with the spouse ("He/she is the only one who understands me"). Similar idealizing (or transference) within an individual treatment experience encourages further projection onto the partner, produces splitting of ambivalent feelings into love for the therapist and hate for the partner, and leads to a spiraling descent into greater frustration and pain. However, if the individual therapist launches a too vigorous challenge of projections, this may lead to the disruption of the fragile alliance, with a patient leaving therapy convinced that one more person could not be trusted to understand.

Encouraging the patient to invite the partner into the session is frequently an effective way to avert these grim alternatives. Abuses of transference are less frequent. With the spouse present, the person previously in individual treatment can be encouraged to try out his perceptions and negotiating skills. The leverage for change is markedly en-

hanced as the partners deal with one another rather than
one individual presenting his perception of the other, necessarily relying on memories. This allows the therapist to
be in the position of helping both partners discover a shared
reality rather than being an arbitrary interpreter of reality.
   Not every spouse needs to be brought into the treatment
scene by a skilled individual therapist; rather, it is a strategy that is available to the clinician and often provides satisfying results.

   A second pattern of individual therapy for marital difficulties is reflected in the common situation of a couple,
both of whom define themselves as emotionally ill, seeing
separate individual therapists. Projection and triangulation
are invited by such arrangements, as partners can use their
respective therapists as mouthpieces for their efforts to control one another. "My daddy can whip your daddy," easily becomes, "My psychotherapist is smarter than yours."
This awkward and complex system can be short-circuited
and simplified by direct communication between the spouses, assisted by one therapist. This is also preferable to having the individual psychotherapists get together, with over-
tones of parents struggling to control squabbling offspring.
(Recent cartoon shows the wife, lying in bed with her husband, saying, "My analyst says that your analyst need analysis.") Gurman and Kniskern, in a summary of psychotherapeutic outcome studies, report that when a person
comes into treatment complaining of marital problems, a
therapist can expect much better results with marital therapy
than with individual treatment. The marital approach shows
improvement in 66% of cases, compared to 40% with individual psychotherapy. Further, and quite important, the
frequency of bad results for the individuals (hospitalization,
suicide attempts, psychotic reactions) is only one-fourth as
frequent with the marital approach (30).

Case Example. Dr. E., a 45-year-old dentist, entered individual treatment because he was depressed and felt hopeless. Bored with his career, unable to enjoy his wife, isolated from his children, he placed total responsibility for his sad state in his wife's lap. *She* wouldn't let him consider other ways of making a living; *she* alienated his children from him; *she* criticized his eating and drinking habits; *she* hounded him to get other interests. Almost every statement began with, "She says I . . . ." He initiated a brief separation, then returned home but in treatment sessions continued the litany of helplessness and impotence against a controlling woman. After Dr. E. rebuffed many attempts to encourage him to define his wishes and desires for himself, the therapist suggested that he invite his wife into the sessions, since she seemed to be the most powerful person in the room, whether present in body or in spirit.

She appeared. A thin, anxious, fragile but attractive woman, she seemed to welcome the opportunity to tell her own story of frustration and hopelessness in a house full of children with an unhappy husband who seemed more afraid of his mother than of her. The reality was much easier for the therapist and Dr. E. to deal with than the nightmarish projection had ever been.

A third indication for couples therapy can be stated by taking the above illustration a bit further: when a person seeking help from a psychotherapist describes his or her problems primarily in terms of marital difficulty.

A fourth indication for couples therapy grows out of a family evaluation usually related to a child's being defined as emotionally ill. Family therapists are skilled at seeing the whole family together, redefining or "reframing" the child's difficulties as related to the family system, and making systems interventions. Often, however, couples treatment is preferable to regular whole family sessions. The choice may be for practical, logistical reasons, as when children are away at school or in different schools. Sometimes it is a result of the therapist's preference. The therapist can utilize systems thinking and systems intervention with varied combinations of patients and others. For example, in an unruly, poorly behaved, hostile family, I prefer to work with the couple rather than with the whole family, as I do not enjoy the constant limit-setting required with these children. There are also sound theoretical reasons. The Timberlawn research showed a close correlation between the parental coalition's competence and satisfaction and the whole family's functioning ability. From clinical work, it is usual that children's emotional problems clear up if the couple's conflicts are better resolved.

A therapist may rationally choose to intervene in the family system by intensive work with the couple, expecting that improvement in the marital coalition will be reflected in greater family satisfaction and reduced symptoms of the identified patient within that family. When the focus of the family is on the behavior or symptoms of a child, the therapist can effectively serve as a consultant to the couple and help them parent more successfully.

Case Example. A pediatrician had been treating 11-year-old James H. for behavior problems in school. James had been diagnosed as having hypoglycemia and hyperactivity syndrome, but diet and medication had produced little improvement in school performance or behavior at home. The pediatrician suspected family problems and requested that the whole family present themselves to the therapist.

Mr. H. was a 48-year-old plant worker with a previous marriage and two grown children. In the consultation room, he was submissive, servile, and obviously anxious. Mrs. H., a 45-year-old secretary, also previously married, appeared wary of her husband and solicitous of James, her son. James and Mary were Mrs. H.'s children by her previous marriage. The boy seemed curious, rather calm, and able to talk easily of his problems in the classroom and his fear of his stepfather. Mary, age 15, spoke cheerfully of her school activities and of her perception that things were all right at home. Mr. and Mrs. H. had been married for five years. Mrs. H. was, on the whole, more satisfied in this relationship than she had been in her previous marriage. Mr. H., she said, was aggressive, and this was seen as a great improvement over her indolent and unhelpful first spouse. However, Mr. H.'s efforts at disciplining her two children, especially James, seemed to her harsh and frightening. Mr. H. defensively said she always asked him to help with the children but nothing he did suited her. He, in turn, felt that she ignored him and favored James.

An obvious problem area was the confused and frustrated expectations these parents had of each other. Since James seemed a reasonably intact 11-year-old, the therapist recommended couples therapy. A practical advantage of this approach was that it avoided a disturbance in school attendance that regular family therapy would have required. Work began with the stated purpose of helping the parents enjoy their relationship with James and helping him function better. His hypoglycemia and hyperactivity disappeared as the parents began to focus on their needs for each other and their difficulty in satisfying those needs.

A further indication for couples therapy is acute psychosis, severe depression, or acute drug or alcohol abuse in a marital partner assigned to outpatient treatment. In such a crisis situation, drug treatment and individual psychotherapy often are not enough, and mobilizing a supportive environment can make the difference between treatment success and failure. Working within the traditional narrowly defined medical model (with the person in crisis labeled as ill) allows an entrée into the couple's relationship that can provide the needed help from the spouse for the patient and the practitioner, while setting the stage for more intensive work once the acute illness has dissipated.

Case Example. Mr. T., a 40-year-old administrator, had been experimenting with illicit hallucinogens for some time. After one drug experience, he became acutely psychotic, with bizarre behavior in his office that frightened his secretary. He believed himself to be in touch with God, possessing intense awareness of all the universe, and was trying vainly to communicate his new-found knowledge to others. Neither he nor his wife wished him to be hospitalized, and the wife appeared willing, intelligent, concerned, and capable of helping in this crisis. It was the judgment of the therapist to institute treatment at home and to visit the couple daily. Along with antipsychotic medication and individual psychotherapy, couples work provided an opportunity for Mr. T. to reenter a relationship with his wife, and for Mrs. T. to reduce her anxiety about what was happening and how she could help. After two weeks, the psychosis abated and office visits were possible.

(Such severe episodes are not routinely treatable without hospitalization, of course, and if a significant possibility of suicide is suspected, the burden on the family may be too great to be handled in this fashion.)

WHEN COUPLES THERAPY IS CONTRAINDICATED

A contraindication for ongoing couples work is the lack of a stated desire on the part of both people to see whether they can evolve a satisfying relationship. Successful psychotherapy of any sort requires some minimal investment in a shared project and a conscious desire to explore and experiment with the possibilities in the relationship necessary for productive change. This requirement is to be sharply distinguished from a commitment to the marriage at the outset.

Ambivalence, leading to internal conflict, is a legacy of being human. Our imperfect world is populated by clumsy and inept humans stumbling over their own feet as they reach for one another. Even in satisfactory relationships there are unmet yearnings and dreams that give partners pause when asked to make a blanket commitment forestalling possible alternatives.

The requirement for entering couples treatment is only to recognize the ambivalence and to consider solutions that

do not preclude investing in the partner. When such a conscious commitment cannot be made, it usually reflects clo-
sure on the part of one person, a resolution already formed
to leave the relationship. No one can make someone care
or gain absolution from another for personal choice. People are so often trying to do things that cannot be done,
becoming horribly frustrated without knowing why. The
therapist can easily model the same kind of hopeless effort
if he ignores this requirement for a commitment to work
together. Negotiation with the couple on this issue can provide needed experience in reaching attainable goals.

Many troubled people come into couples work with either/
or alternatives, both of which are unacceptable; for example,
"I must *either* divorce *or* commit to a bad relationship." Offering a third, more attainable alternative—to acknowledge
unresolved ambivalence and to move toward its resolution—
is often the beginning of a more satisfactory life for both people, whether that resolution is to part or to stay together.

Case Example. Mr. and Mrs. D., ages 29 and 30, referred themselves after hearing the therapist present a talk on family and
couples therapy. Mrs. D. had filed for divorce, and Mr. D. was
adamantly against it. Mrs. D. declared she was not in love with
him and was contemptuous of his sexual performance—or, more
precisely, his relative lack of sexual interest. She had agreed to
come in with her husband, but could not conjure up any fantasy
of his changing to become a desirable partner. Mr. D. was referred
for individual therapy, and then Mrs. D. accepted the offer of psychotherapy to help her do whatever she wanted to do, since she
was clear on only one point—that her husband was undesirable.

In the ensuing months, she did not divorce, but continued a
series of affairs that initially she endowed with great romantic
hopes. In time she saw these as pointless and distasteful to her.
There were many advantages to her married state (such as financial security and social position) that she was loath to give up, and
she found herself hungering to love the person she lived with.
She decided that she wished to work with her husband to see if

she could clear up her unresolved feelings toward him. Though she was still not certain that she could love Mr. D., she decided to rid herself of extramarital activities and invite her husband into treatment to determine whether communicating her desires more effectively would develop the relationship into a satisfactory one for her. Only after long and arduous individual work on her part did the therapist agree that couples treatment would be a good investment of time, energy, and money.

For a partner who cannot commit to an exploration of the relationship with an open mind, individual work is indicated. Sometimes months in psychotherapy will be necessary to bring this individual to the point of decision—to divorce or to see whether the marriage will work.

The above contraindication is related only to couples therapy. There can be divorce therapy in which either or neither partner wishes to continue the relationship; the context then can be quite clear as to the therapist's responsibility to help the members of a disintegrating partnership to understand and utilize the experience. There also can be consultation with spouses who are unsure what they wish to work on; this will be a short-lived intervention, usually no more than one session, with the focus on assisting each to express himself or herself more clearly. It is not helpful to extend the consultation period when one person is unable to make the minimal commitment of seeing whether the relationship could be enjoyable. One of two undesirable things will happen. Either the openly ambivalent partner, with no underlying intent to attempt the healing of the relationship, will launch a no-holds-barred attack on the other, or the covertly ambivalent partner will keep quiet and avoid those mixed feelings that must be addressed.

A second contraindication for couples therapy is a highly invested ongoing affair or sexual relationship with a lover (of the same or opposite sex) that one partner desires to continue and reveals to the therapist but does not wish to reveal to the spouse. Mistrust is at the core of painful, frustrating relationships, and the therapist must be trustworthy in fact, not just in theory. If he knows a powerful secret about one partner that relates to the success or failure of the spouses' daily interaction, and the secret is not to be shared, he is not trustable and will provide for both partners a further experience in an untrustworthy environment encouraging despair and projection. If the spouse knows of the liaison, the therapist can be trusted and the couple can proceed toward the goal of mutual satisfaction for both. Further, this caveat applies only to current extramarital romantic and/or sexual bonds. Past events are the property of the individuals involved, and whether they are shared or not is a decision of the owners of the memories, not of the therapist.

I believe that affairs can hold stuck marriages together probably as often as they rip them asunder. If reasonably gratifying, the affair may avert emotional illness in the involved spouse. But it is my clinical observation that a couple's relationship cannot be improved while such a liaison continues, since nobody—partners or therapist—can determine with reasonable confidence whether a given complaint is to be taken at face value or understood as a displacement from the events transpiring in the affair. The results of trying to sort out confused motives are uniformly poor.

It is a powerful and highly significant step for two people to share with a therapist their effort to find emotional and sexual satisfaction; this work surely must be taken seriously by all concerned. An experienced professional knows how difficult such a task is and must not allow the shared effort to be burdened with impossible ambiguities.

A consistent observation in family systems research is the confused, muddy context found in disturbed families, with children in the role of parents, adults competing with children, and misdirection and avoidance of personal responsibility. Competent families, by contrast, have a marvelously clear contextual base, firm generational boundaries, and openness in dealing with inevitable conflicts. Renunciation is a necessary part of finding satisfaction in finite human interaction. Children who declare, at age four, that they will marry daddy or mommy when they grow up, learn, as they grow older, that they can have a parent and a lover, but not both in the same person. Accepting limits is necessary to attain intimacy. Psychotherapists must model clarity and limits as they help troubled people learn that they can have a lover and a therapist but not both in the same person. They also model this clarity with regard to outside relationships by stating, "I don't think I can help you develop intimacy with your spouse if you are seeking a similar goal with your lover. You may wish to continue this unsatisfying marriage because of power, position, children, or other reasons, and find what intimacy you can elsewhere. That is surely a respectable and perhaps viable choice. But if you wish to promote growth in your life with your spouse, letting go of the lover will be necessary in order not to become entrapped in unresolved ambivalence."

The above is not a parental or judgmental statement, but that of a battle-scarred therapist providing a model of doing the possible by clarifying and accepting limits. In this or similar issues, the treatment effort must point toward helping resolve ambivalence and encouraging growth. Ignoring the above-mentioned contextual aspects of a psychotherapist's role will often lead to such poor results that a therapist may be driven back into the relatively simple, safe, but limited strategy of individual work. Careful attention to the contextual will reduce the risks inherent in more complex systems of intervention.

 A third, very occasional, contraindication consists of an overt, pervasive, and disruptive paranoid orientation on the part of one partner toward the other. One spouse's motives are continually viewed as malignant, and every interaction provides fresh evidence of the other's evil purposes. The therapist's observation that perhaps the behavior can be interpreted in several different ways is construed as an attack; thus frightened, the globally mistrustful partner will include the therapist along with the spouse as having malevolent intent. In such a situation, couples work should be abandoned and efforts made to arrange for individual treatment for one or both of the people involved.

To make this contraindication clear, I wish to distinguish between the ordinary projections seen in every troubled couple and the peculiar variety of projection properly called paranoid. Most couples have areas of their behavior viewed as the miserable result of willful, purposeful sabotaging by the other, but their accusations are spotty and inconsistent. The truly paranoid defense is certain, global, and not open to negotiation. Behavior of the other person is perceived as clearly evil. Further, the paranoid thoughts are pervasive.

In discouraging couples work in such a situation, I do not suggest that the mutual interaction is not a major contributor to the problem. Quite the contrary, I have yet to see a couple with a paranoid partner in which the other person is not extremely ambiguous and indirect in communicating thoughts and feelings. The systems problem will be evident, but couples intervention at this juncture will probably fail.

OTHER TREATMENT MODES USED IN CONJUNCTION WITH COUPLES STRATEGY

There are no insurmountable problems in working with an individual in intensive psychotherapy while relating to him and his partner in conjoint treatment. The individually treated spouse may feel one-down because of the implicit label "sick." The spouse who sees the therapist only as part of the couple unit may feel left out or discriminated against. However, these issues can be resolved through negotiation and discussion. When I see one person, I am his agent; when I see two, I am the agent of both. Further, I have confidence that if they see each other as needful humans, each one's needs will be compatible with the other's, since resolved ambivalence, responsible choice, and clarity are so much easier to deal with than are their alternatives.

Defining my role clearly in the two different contexts usually allows the spouse seen less frequently to develop trust that I am fair and do not play favorites; the exceptions to this occur especially in situations where the individual work began long before the couples came together. Here another therapist may be necessary.

There is an intrinsic problem, however, in seeing both partners separately in addition to the couples work over an extended time. Central to all emotional and relationship difficulties is a problem of trust. The troubled spouses have had difficulty trusting each other sufficiently, and prolonged periods of individual work with any two people who live under the same roof makes well-nigh impossible demands on each of them to trust the motives of the therapist, especially during particularly trying periods for the couple. Individual work invites positive and negative transference fantasies that, when linked to the competitiveness and rivalry often evidenced by the pair, can overwhelm the most straightforward and open therapist.

The administration of psychoactive drugs to one member of the pair is certainly feasible. In order to avoid a blurred role for the therapist, however, medications should be given with the same orientation of partnership and shared power experienced in couples work. In *Psychotherapy and Growth*, a text on treatment, I present this egalitarian model of drug therapy in more detail (5). Unlike organic treatments such as electroshock, the administration of drugs can be accomplished either in the traditionally powerful style of the physician or in an egalitarian mode with the patient equally responsible for decisions as to whether, when, and how medicine is taken.

③ Group therapy for one or both partners is frequently a most useful augmentation to couple strategy, especially with couples who have a "gruesome twosome" orientation—that is, couples who, though thoroughly dissatisfied with each other, nevertheless cling together because the outside world seems even more threatening. Providing a setting in which partners learn by experience that satisfying intimacies and friendships can add to the pleasure of each other's company, rather than being a dreaded threat, can profoundly alter attitudes of jealousy and possessiveness.

④ Family therapy for couples with children is also frequently useful in conjunction with couples treatment. The therapist, by seeing the whole family initially at least once, can get an insight into family dynamics and make a family assessment that will be valuable for all future work with any part of the family system.

Further, after couples therapy has been going well, bringing other family members, such as children, parents, and grandparents, into the treatment setting can provide new understandings, break deadlocks, and offer needed assistance to the couple and the therapist.

Case Example. Mr. and Mrs. P., ages 36 and 35 respectively, had begun couples work after Mr. P. had been in individual treatment for several months and had gradually focused on some marital problems. Couples work had gone well, with each partner dealing with longings and fears regarding emotional intimacy and developing increasing appreciation for a "systems orientation," that is, realizing that each person is a part of the problem and solution and that each has influence with the other but cannot control the other. As they began work on some parenting issues, they were invited to bring in the whole family—themselves and their three sons, ages nine, seven, and five. No one of these children was defined as emotionally ill, but all were seen as having problems, such as high anxiety, learning difficulties, and dishonesty. After several sessions, both parents agreed that the children were really less troubled than they were, and the couple strategy was reinstituted. Mr. P.'s parents from another state came to visit and were invited to a session. In part of the interview, Mr. P.'s mother told of the death of Mr. P.'s brother and of his becoming anorexic soon after, at the age of five and a half. The reciting of these events, which had been thoroughly repressed by Mr. P., sharply increased his awareness of the emotional hunger, denial, and efforts at control that had influenced the couple's relationship patterns.

conflict = ambivalence

in couple/family   in individual

2 IMPORTANT SYSTEMS CONCEPTS AND ISSUES

AT THE INDIVIDUAL SYSTEMS LEVEL

The family level and the individual level of systems are intimately related. Children grow up with conscious and unconscious perceptions of themselves, ideas about male and female roles, strategies of relating, and views of the world outside. Their views are a result of absorbing the family experience, its rules and assumptions expressed in action. Watching whole families interact, I often feel like a voyeur peeking into the next generation's individual intrapsychic structure.

For example, conflict, ubiquitous in families (or any other human group), is isomorphic (structurally similar) with the ambivalence found in another system, the individual human being. Conflict in a family or between marital partners is no more pathological than is ambivalence in one individual. These are givens in the business of being human.

Ambivalence

Ambivalence arises out of a human biological reality: We have this dramatically overgrown frontal cortex (in comparison to other species) that, acting in conjunction with our lively midbrain allows—nay forces—dreams and fantasies—beauty not yet seen, perfection never encountered, lovers never experienced. Such a capacity to dream is rudely chal-

29

lenged and frustrated, brought to earth, by experiences in a world where rains defile picnics, mothers have tantrums, lovers become obese and have varicose veins.

Like individual ambivalence, conflict in a family group is inescapable, with each person being an independent single source sending out messages of hunger, need, frustration, anger, and love that are not immediately or easily orchestrated with the signals from other family members. An infant crying with hunger or loneliness at midnight while a tired mother is in the arms of the father dramatically illustrates this kind of ubiquitous conflict.

There is a significant, promising, and frustrating chicken-and-egg quality to these two phenomena—ambivalence and family conflict—that is central to an effective approach to couples treatment. The two actors in the couple's drama come together from quite different family systems and intrapsychic family structures, no matter how similar their backgrounds may be. The more each person has experienced family conflict as negotiable, the more that person has learned that individual ambivalence is resolvable. In a similar way, the more each person brings to the relationship the capacity to resolve ambivalence and proceed autonomously, the more they can successfully negotiate in the couple relationship and later within a larger family group.

On the other hand, the more a member of a couple has been raised in a family where unresolved conflict has festered and impaired family functioning, the more difficulty that person has in resolving his own individual ambivalence about significant relationships. Such an individual is quite likely to seek out a partner with a similar degree of difficulty in resolving ambivalence and achieving committed intimacy. Together they create a new family with a strong probability of chronic unresolvable conflict. Conversely, the more fortunate individuals who grew up in families where differences were usually resolved learn to make decisions and choices and usually select a partner with similar skills. They are unlikely to require psychotherapy.

Working with disturbed families or individuals, we see parents who cannot resolve their internal ambivalence developing unresolvable conflict in their families, to the detriment of all family members' functioning. A couples therapist is not called upon to favor individual choice over dyadic or family good; neither is he to invest in the family at the expense of individual autonomy and choice. Rather, these are interacting, reciprocal aspects of a given system; the freedom of one person is also freedom for the other. When one person has more dignity, the system rules allow the other equal dignity. Opposition between individual and group (whether couple, family or society) is a false dichotomy, found in disturbed families and in primitive theory. If one member of a couple learns to recognize, accept, and resolve his own ambivalence, the family or couple system benefits. Any member of the team of couple and therapist can model the resolution of ambivalence and develop responsible choice, with resulting benefit for all.

Case Example. I once accepted for couples treatment a mental health professional and his wife who had been through years of psychoanalysis. After four or five interviews it became apparent that each was committed to acting out engrained attitudes and behaviors: she being hostile and outrageously aggressive; he, silky smooth, long-suffering and implicitly contemptuous. It was painful to be in the same room with them, and though I wanted to be useful, I felt I was getting nowhere. I resolved this conflict by saying, ''I quit! Though you both suffer terribly, neither of you will end the battle. I will show you how; I refuse to see you anymore.'' I sent them to a respected colleague who perhaps was more gentle than I, but they did divorce. Several years later, they both had done well as individuals, and the ex-husband told me that he appreciated what I had done but disapproved of the way I had done it. It was, however, the only way I knew then (or know now) to model the resolution of ambivalence and hence to intervene effectively in that particular instance.

The acceptance of ambivalence as a normal condition leads to the capacity to resolve it and *choose*. Choice-making is a basic expression of our unique and special selfhood; a good case can be made that it is only through choice that individuals exist at all. Our choices are clearly limited by our biology and by the capricious circumstances of birth and later experiences, but they are a part of us. When choice is denied, there is great risk of suffering and emotional illness.

Nevertheless, many if not most people and families deny the reality of choice every day. And some theoreticians promote concepts of determinism, fixed biological drives and external control (27). The wry aphorism, "When adversity comes, take it like a man, blame it on your wife," captures the flavor of this human tendency to avoid the responsibility inherent in being alive, that is, the responsibility of making personal choices. Avoidance of choice can be seen as an elemental part of human emotional illness. Regression, transference, projection, behavior that forces societal controls— are all methods to confuse ourselves. We evade the loneliness of individuality and lose the gratification experienced through choosing.

The term "vector," defined here as "force with direction," is a useful concept in evaluating competence in individuals and families. Emotionally disturbed people cannot move symbolically (and often physically) in any consistent direction; psychosis, sociopathy, and/or severe depression prevent effective commitment to people, ideas, career, hobbies. Activity comes to a standstill or shoots off erratically in alternating, opposing directions.

Case Example. I once cared for an acutely disturbed woman suffering from catatonic schizophrenia who vividly illustrated this concept. As I approached the door of her room, she would take three steps toward me, stop, take three steps back, and stop. She would repeat the cycle until I left. She wanted to move toward me, to make closer contact, and then, too fearful, she retreated. Her behavior was a concrete expression of a similar lack of resolved choice found in the members of severely disturbed couples. Often neither can admit that they wish to live together, nor can they face life alone. The phenomenon also can be seen in whole families. Presented with a task such as "Plan something together," conflict-ridden families drift aimlessly and fruitlessly, unable to choose.

Less disturbed, but still emotionally handicapped, individuals try to be effective by repressing one side of powerful opposing feelings, thus moving in a consistent direction but without the subjective experience of choice. They stay with jobs or spouses for years, though behaviorally indicating negative feelings about their situation. Hives pop out, stomach linings ulcerate, arterioles hypertrophy, diffuse anxiety or truculence evolves, but nothing is done to find a more gratifying life.

There is no gratification without choice. This is a one-liner I often use in clinical work. An important therapeutic task is to assist emotionally suffering people in becoming aware of and sorting out their mixed feelings in order that they can choose a direction representing most of their personhood rather than just the portion acceptable to present or past family roles. Working with couples is one strategy to facilitate the achievement of these goals. The concrete stated task is to help two people decide whether they wish to live together and then discover ways to do so, but in the process individual skills in choosing and attaining are developed, whetted and honed.

Case Example. An executive came to treatment acutely suicidal. Married twenty years to a wife he had come to regard as domineering and personally unappealing, though he still admired her intelligence and confidence, he had a lengthy affair with a married woman who "turned him on" to sex, to fantasy, to intense passion. After she broke off the sexual part of the relationship, pleading guilt over continuing sex outside of marriage, he became progressively more depressed. His painful bind was one of indecision as to whether he wanted to leave his wife or try to develop with her something of the relationship he had experienced with his mistress. For several months after the affair ended, he and his wife had visited a marriage counselor. In this context he behaved like a turned worm. Previously meek and passive, he now complained loudly and made demands. His wife responded and altered her ways considerably, which only frustrated him more, as he felt no closer, no more loving. It was at this point that he became suicidal. Having separated his fantasy life and his real relationships to the breaking point, his first treatment goal was a decision as to whether to try to find gratification in marriage or to divorce. We began by looking at the real attributes he saw in his mistress and exploring possibilities he believed to be present in his wife. He soon became aware that each woman had good and bad features. With this perspective came the realization of being genuinely afraid to venture out by himself, at which point couples therapy was indicated. His efforts to resolve ambivalence and experience the choices that were possible could then bear fruit.

Projection

In my clinical practice the main stumbling block to resolving ambivalence for troubled people is the pesky use of projection, that is, experiencing feelings which originate within the self as coming from outside, a fundamental breakdown of self boundaries. As we shall see in later chapters, much of the work in couples therapy centers around reducing or eliminating projective phenomena and clarifying the boundaries between family members. Without such clarity, potentially resolvable *internal* conflicts are experienced as unresolvable conflicts *between people*, and the most frequent person chosen for such chronic displacement is a lover or spouse.

This kind of projective activity is seductively attractive for many reasons: First and foremost, it eliminates the terrible anxiety of ambivalence. Though the battle is merely shifted (in perception) from an internal source to an external one, the threat to the integrity of the self is removed. Fighting an external enemy, though unrewarding, at least provides the illusion of internal peace and security. A broad analogy may clarify. In the simpler days of World War II, the shared perception of the bad guys "out there" made our population feel closer and warmer toward one another. The Vietnamese War, by contrast, found us a consciously divided people, ambivalent, uncertain and worried about the integrity and survival of our country. The perceived external threat, though deadly, was experienced as less painful than the internal conflict and threat to our identity.

Secondly, projection makes issues spuriously simple. *If only* the spouse would shape up—become more glamorous, more loving, less hostile, more interesting, less controlling— my life would be fine.

Further, if I project to a socially acceptable object, for instance, spouse, children, or parents, I can find buddies who will agree. Another woman will usually believe that my wife doesn't understand me, or other angry, frustrated parents will understand that I have ungrateful children. My homely projections enable me to feel less alone than my groping efforts to direct my life.

The degree to which people use projection is not the important variable in a definition of mental illness. Individuals often describe personal disappointments intensely and pervasively explained by their spouses' obstinate behavior. No paranoid schizophrenic uses more projection than such people. The difference between the sane and the insane is not the amount, but the kind. If I project consistently and openly onto objects that seem to others only tangentially related to me, such as the CIA, strangers, or an old boss that I haven't seen in years, I will seem bizarre. But if I keep the projections directed at personally close people in my life, I will never blow my cover—people won't realize that I don't exist at all as a functioning self. However, when a couples therapist begins to deal with those who have learned this trick, that is, looking normal while denying personal existence and responsibility through projection, the similarity between these people and frank schizophrenics becomes painfully clear. The therapist who challenges projections produces profound anxiety and threat to experienced identity.

If I blame my spouse for my problems, I am still considered a responsible member of society. My brother who blames the FBI for his problems and is locked up may not be as different from me in ego strength as our relative social power would indicate. Psychiatric data and discussions concerning narcissistic personalities and borderline conditions present an evolving challenge to any comfortable dichotomy between the sane and the crazy. Important developmental issues point to a continuum. Therapists will be more accurate in their assessments if they look at how people operate and what mechanisms they use, rather than simply categorizing them on the content of their behavior.

Why projection? What onerous emotional burden begins the process of laying blame, destroying boundaries, promoting endless interpersonal battles? Why do apparently sane people devote their energies to avoiding responsibilities rather than reaching for a satisfying life? A short foray into concepts of family and child development can help us here.

Family Dynamics and Child Development

An infant enters a family with a capacity for empathic relating. As growth occurs with experience, its developing nervous system makes ever finer discriminations and the symbolic self—the mystical "I"—evolves. A body ego is first delineated: When I bite my toe it hurts, and when I bite the sheet it doesn't. Then the "me" must be discriminated from the nurturer; with awareness of boundaries comes fear of loss as I realize that the people I need are not within me and I can't magically control them.

There follows a stage of development on the way to separation and individuation usually termed symbiosis (37), a normal phase of human interaction when emerging boundaries are filled with projective phenomena. If adult family members and older siblings have successfully mastered this developmental period, each helps the child wrestle with the ubiquitous human ambivalence of bad me/good me, bad mama/good mama. With increasing acceptance of the world and oneself as a "mixed bag," choices can be experienced in the context of an imperfect but satisfying world. Trust then moves from the necessary absolute trust of an infant to the relative trust of a consciously separate, vulnerable human who is capable of loneliness, fear, and rage and who can move toward his own personally defined satisfaction.

In many families, however, the child encounters parents who themselves have had no assistance in moving through this symbiotic period. They still project their presumed inadequacies onto others, blaming parents, siblings, or spouses for their frustrations. The hoped-for "cogwheeling" described by Erik Erikson (22), the productive and happy meeting of developmental capacity and family environmental opportunities, does not occur, and this person becomes an adult with blurred boundaries, who by frequent use and experience of blame and projection eliminates from consciousness parts of the self by projection.

H. S. Sullivan spoke of the "not me" as the part of the self rejected by significant others—a shadow part of the person unclaimed and poised for projection onto others (46). Each of us has some of this "not me"; our family experiences are paramount in determining its proportions. Does it include anger? Or self-pity? Or sexual desire? Is one most afraid of being seen as helpless or as bad? Look to the original family for the pattern of the self, its open and closed areas.

Guilt

Guilt in individuals is related to hiddenness from others. The more I believe I must hide from my parents, my siblings, my friends, my lover, the more of me that remains "not me," a source of guilt whether conscious or unconscious. A family system made up of developmentally stunted people, with shaky boundaries frequently utilizing projection, sets the stage for the next generation to grow up, marry, and continue their own recreation of scarred selves. This concept provides both the sense of titanic struggle and the satisfaction in working with couples, for each step forward made by this pair in recognizing and accepting their individual selves means less projection to the spouse or children, present or yet unborn.

A couples therapist can invite the two to "grow themselves up," to further separate and individuate and leave the stuck position of symbiosis behind. In the process, each will have less neurotic guilt, a greater awareness of his/her own complexity, and more intimate knowledge of the other.

Boundary Disturbances

There are several recurrent themes with people who have poor boundary definitions. These include fear of going berserk and destroying others, fear of sexual misconduct, fear of the person or things projected on, fear of being swallowed, and a strange sense of emptiness.

Fears of sexual and aggressive possibilities are easily understood as emanating from being taught that such feelings are evil and, if not repressed, a path to self-destruction. Believing that, then one will avoid personal choice and look for people and circumstances to pin down and control. "Loving means controlling" is the rule of such a person, following his family of origin. It is a usual family belief of the large group of families I have described as "midrange" (7, 13).

With this definition of the self as basically evil, and with the search for control predominant, rescuers and persecutors become the same people. They bedevil the victim, but the victim will play the same intimidating role for the rescuer/persecutors and so these definitions go around and around as in a bad soap opera.

To live a satisfying life requires close relationships where one is known and accepted. Unfortunately, these are often avoided for fear of being swallowed, engulfed, taken over—of becoming nobody. Emotional and sometimes physical distance can be experienced as the only way to maintain the tenuous existence of the self. The gutsy, juicy qualities of anger, sex, human hunger, even tenderness, projected onto others create a potential threat in getting close to anyone. When these powerful qualities are projected, the self is experienced as flat and empty, like an abandoned house. Fantasy is either barren or drearily repetitive. Successful playing out of narrow family self-definitions results in feeling less than half alive. When such people in treatment can claim their own feelings, the surge of energy and self-assessed capability is striking.

Case Example. Some 20 years ago, Mr. and Mrs. Y. came into treatment ostensibly for sexual problems; both defined him as a premature ejaculator. Both were quite wary of each other, not trusting feeling statements and fearful of honest expression. He had a family with a hardworking father, rarely at home, and a depressed mother who clung to her son out of loneliness. This encouraged Mr. Y. to identify closeness with estrangement. Mrs. Y. had grown up in a family with both parents working together in a small

business; she felt herself to be an unnecessary burden and intimacy, though longed for, was thought to be fraudulent when
available.

Over a period of 10 months, this couple experienced a series
of honest encounters in the office, and they learned their fears
were unfounded. They left with a new sense of mutual tenderness
and joy that was infectious.

In subsequent years, they have had losses—the death of a child;
the serious depression of her father. Though they have returned
for help with these crises, their trust in each other has been maintained.

Sexual Identity

Particular aspects of the projected self related to sexual
identity are seen with great regularity in clinical practice (8).
Males often feel obliged to place fear, loneliness, tenderness
and affection in the denied category. Females more frequently suffer from denied power wishes; assertiveness is surrounded by guilt, and competence may seem nearly obscene.
This cultural handicap, duly transmitted by the family tem-
plate, provides ready material for projection to be played
out by the partner. As the husband tries to be a Roman cen-
turion, he fears his wife's clutching dependency, never noting his own needs for her. As the wife attempts to be a supportive helpmate, subjugating her ambitions as a person,
she feels trapped by his directive, insensitive control, the
same control that she has abdicated for her own life.

The foregoing composite description of a male/female
system suggests the complex interplay between cultural expectations, character patterns, projections, and self-fulfilling
prophecies. Each person feeds cues to the other that perpetuate repetitive, unsatisfying, undesired responses and
patterns. To describe such patterns as characterological will
produce the old-fashioned labels of individual sickness, e.g.,
"depressed hysteric" or "compulsive neurotic." But it is

in the circularity of the pattern, the unconscious triggering of predictable responses by the partner's previous response, that the major possibilities for treatment reside.

Human Qualities Unacceptable to Varied Family Types

In clinical and research activities, working with families of different degrees of competence and dysfunction, I began to formulate a pattern of underlying assumptions as most important in understanding the contents of the hidden self. Midrange families—those that may be expected to produce sane but limited offspring, the wellspring of neurotics and moderate behavior disorders—believe the nature of man to be evil and specifically antisocial, leading to sexual misconduct and aggressive/destructive behavior unless the person is controlled by the forces of civilization. Those same forces became "civilized" by denying their basic "evil" . . . and so on back to Adam and Eve.

Members of more disturbed families agree that people are basically evil, but they disagree as to how this evil came about and exactly what it is. Severely disturbed families clinging together, distrusting the outside world, define people's basic evil as disloyalty expressed by the stubborn desire to be free of the family's intertwined controls of mutual obligation. Since the need for an individual identity, for personal choice, is a developmental drive, it follows that disturbed families interpret this striving as evidence of basic perversity. Another kind of severely disturbed family defines basic human evil as weakness, the desire for love and affection expressed as clinging. In these families we see only a fragment of nurturing and members try desperately to find satisfaction and identity in the world outside.

The common theme in these frequently distorted views is the definition as basically evil of that which is useful and respectable in some context. It is not the human quality itself.

but the attempt to stamp it out that produces destructiveness.

The Nature of Truth

In addition to the denied part of the self used in projection, another individual characteristic evolved from family
rules can make personal choice difficult or impossible. Individuals often believe that truth is absolute—not relative,
not subjective, but objective and clear to anyone of virtue
and good sense. I have termed this belief, "my eye as God's
eye." Its logic is as follows. When I believe something, it
is *true*; if you disagree, you challenge my very existence and
I must force you to change by any means or eliminate you
from my life. When I make a decision, it must be *the* right
one or it is completely wrong. If my decision to marry is correct, that marriage must never founder; if it does, it means
either that I am emotionally bankrupt by being wrong or that
I was betrayed by some unworthy other.

This view of truth is a primitive one, historically and
developmentally. A chaotic state creates a yearning for certainty, however spurious. In families whose members have
progressed beyond this position, a child can experience ambiguity in life and relationships and watch others accept and
deal with it. If, however, parents are unskilled in handling
subjectivity, ambivalence, and uncertainty, the child will be
handicapped in his or her own emotional development. He
or she learns the family process of attack/blame, defensiveness, and justification through an objectified family "referee"—an abstracted set of "shoulds" and "oughts" that
supersedes human negotiation (5).

Every family has at least a few basic beliefs and rules that
must go unchallenged by its members, but the more these
beliefs and rules proliferate and are not subject to negotiation, the more the family offers a Procrustean bed to its
members, cutting off vital aspects of their being and teach-

ing falsely that ambivalence and uncertainty are sinful or sick.

Subjective Truth

In working with disturbed couples, I am struck with how frequently their belief in "objectivity" can diminish their chances for enjoying each other. One partner may say, "We haven't had sex but twice in the last six months." The other responds, "Why that's ridiculous! We have had sex at least once a week." An ugly argument begins with a spiral of vituperation. One works to get such partners to listen to each other and to entertain the possibility that each is telling a very important truth. The experience of sex only twice in six months is probably one of deprivation, of feeling there should be more. "We've had sex once a week" might be translated "I feel like it is a chore; I've done my duty. Get off my back."

Sometimes telling a story and asking for responses from the couple can help teach subjectivity. For instance, I have used this simple illustration: A small child comes running to his father with saucer eyes, shouting, "There's a dog outside as big as a house." The father says, "Now, stop that lying! There is no dog that is as big as a house!" And he punishes the child with a feeling of virtue. We have only our subjective view of the world. No one possesses objectivity. The best we can do is to process our different views with respect, getting closer to one another by understanding the other's perspective.

This kind of really profound change in the understanding of reality and truth represents maturation and growth that is quite possible for members of disturbed couples. The learning experienced in the couple's relationship can carry over into raising children in a way that eliminates the harsh family referee, encouraging openness and sharing of feelings and perceptions.

Freudian psychoanalytic theorists usually consider the child's superego as harsh, tyrannical and unyielding. Growth and development allow the superego to become, in Fenichel's words, "more amenable to the ego, more plastic, and more sensible" (24). Such a development is possible only in families where subjectivity is respected, where ambivalence is accepted as part of being human, where family negotiation is frequent.

The less fortunate individual, imprisoned by a primitive, punishing superego, buttressed by a harsh family referee system that condemns his personal perceptions and expressions, cannot experience comfort and choice. Projecting the unacceptable feelings seems the only way to avoid overwhelming emotional pain.

Many people with this kind of rigid intrapsychic structure are balanced on a razor's edge—on one side is guilt, and on the other is resentment. Their tyranny of the self is a rule system they also impose on others. Since the possessor of this code cannot live up to it, it is of course impossible for another (who has his own set of expectations) to satisfy its demands either. Sometimes the harsh structure is projected onto the spouse, who is then seen as the family referee impotently railed against long ago. At other times the machinery is used as the standard for the partner's feelings, thoughts and behaviors. Since both members of a couple are involved, the result is either overt capitulation and covert resentment or continued unresolved skirmishes. Either way, a new family referee system evolves to plague the next generation.

The rigid superego, useless for guiding behavior because it attacks basic parts of the personality rather than specific strategies used to attain goals, encourages overt symptomatic depression and/or dramatically paranoid outbursts. A therapist interested in the further growth and development of his patients does well to address himself to making the superego more sensible.

I have a rule of thumb about guilt: It is useful if it doesn't last more than five minutes and produces some change in behavior. I encourage recognition of ambivalence, respect for desires and goals, and learning the skills necessary to attain those goals, all of which are ego functions. If we do our job well, we are so busy with developing ego skills that the punishing shoulds and oughts die by attrition.

The concepts of projection and of transference are closely related. The family referee introjected (put inside one's own head) is an uneasy part of one's own self and ready for projection. With neurotic, guilt-ridden people, I have the strange sensation of another head slightly behind the person that is critical of the feelings being expressed by the visible head. Such visual images have encouraged me to conceptualize the individual unconscious as a faithful representation of the whole family system of the child now grown up. One can see in the intrapsychic conflict the recreation of childhood conflicts between family members. Such a head is easily projected onto partners. When this occurs, one sees ludicrous and pathetic charades: A grown woman treats her husband as a misbehaving four-year-old or conversely acts as if he were Zeus making absolute judgments.

Loss

Perhaps life's hardest task is the acceptance of losses due to biology. We lose loved ones from growth and development, from aging and death. Our relationships are constantly altered by the tick of the biological clock. To engage in endless arguments programmed in our heads from childhood provides a way of denying this stark fact; we can create a fiction, supported by others, that a lover or spouse is just like Daddy or Mom, that a son's or daughter's willfulness and resistance to control are ourselves re-encountered. If we identify rather than parent, we can experience a flawed sense of immortality. Hence we can understand the frequent reluctance of couples to experience themselves as unique, special, right now.

Case Example. A 42-year-old woman had lost her husband from cancer two years previously. She did not adapt well, being depressed, going to few social events, and resisting return to productive work. Three months after widowhood, a distant relative, a middle-aged bachelor, began to court her. The relationship was stormy. Her projections, confused statements, and ambivalence about the relationship were nearly psychotic. When it became apparent that she was continually attempting to see this man as if he had the qualities that she attributed to her dead husband, the therapist confronted her unwillingness to accept his death. With much painful emotion, she told of keeping her husband's clothes and his room intact as much as she could and even wanting her nine-year-old not to let people know of his father's death. As she shared her mourning, the agitation and ambivalence regarding her present suitor subsided.

Case Example. A couple in their early forties came to treatment after both had had much individual psychotherapy. They had a terribly painful marriage, frequent vicious quarrels, and a shared appearance of weary, punch-drunk fighters. They recalled that once they had trusted each other more and the relationship had been better. The constant quarrels began following the cribdeath of their firstborn child. No one had helped these emotionally isolated people to express that loss, and blaming each other seemed to reduce the pain.

Coming close to another not only means our innermost self is exposed, but also forces us to deal with our finiteness, our vulnerable humanness, our fragile mortality. Both experiences can be satisfying, but we may need someone to go with us and touch our shoulder when we are afraid.

AT THE FAMILY SYSTEMS LEVEL

The most striking element present in the interactions of troubled couples is rigidity, the drearily repetitive quality of thrust and counterthrust with no change in pattern. As a farm child, I remember watching with fascination as a chicken encountered a fence blocking its usual path. Though an open gate was 10 feet away, the poor chicken paced five feet back and forth, looking vainly for a way to get to her flock. People with neurotic difficulties enmeshed with similarly handicapped partners remind me of that chicken, responding to novel demands with stereotyped responses that guarantee failure. Though the individuals may have Ph.D.'s, they are no more functional than a chicken without help in "jumping track" and using new methods for new problems. Comprehending this rigidity, the hallmark of marital difficulty, may assist us in understanding why many varied techniques can work; directives, paradoxes, reframing, even the administration of drugs may help a pair jump track and find the gate. The surest way to keep a couple out of trouble, however, is to provide both with an understanding of the current predicament and, in addition, enough skills to deal with the novel, the unusual, in a problem-solving fashion. A more adaptive and flexible family or pair does not develop from simply becoming aware of past mistakes and stereotyped patterns. Necessary learning also includes entirely new ways of negotiating and solving problems.

Systems concepts provide a useful framework from which to offer the needed strategies that healthy families provide their children but which are woefully lacking in other families. Systems approaches focus on stereotyped patterns in relationships rather than assuming rigid and inflexible character structure; thus, couples and therapists can learn new skills without getting bogged down trying to change basic personality. The latter goal is not only difficult or impossible, but also not required for increased satisfaction in living. I know of no personality that cannot succeed, and none that cannot fail. A psychotherapist's job is to help people do well with what biology and previous experience have given them.

Boundaries

Boundaries—between the system and outside and between parts of that system—are highly significant in evaluating and treating couples' difficulties.

Boundary trouble between a couple or family and the outside world comes in essentially two varieties—extremes of insulating and barricading against intrusion from outside or, alternatively, investing so much in the outside world that the boundary is functionally destroyed. An example of the first difficulty is the ''gruesome twosome''—partners who are attempting to obtain all of their emotional needs from each other. They often do well until the birth of a child; at the point, the increase in complexity from dyad to triangle occurs and the relationship goes sour. The wife feels pulled between two loyalties, the husband feels betrayed, and both feel resentful and guilty.

The second kind of boundary difficulty is found in every troubled couple—the lack of adequate separation, individuation and autonomy that is expressed in projective boundary confusion. Confronted by a troubled couple—angry, blaming and justifying—I often fantasize two inept burglars who agree to rob a bank. Everything goes well in the early part of the caper when it is mostly in imagination, but during the break-in both believe they hear sirens. Each begins to rail at the other, accusing the partner of setting off the alarm. All thoughts of getting cash or even making a safe retreat are forgotten. As hopelessness increases, their attacks on each other escalate. At this point I am asked to enter the picture and attempt to help the pair redirect their activities. From their goal of projecting the denied helplessness and ineptness onto the other and desperately trying to stamp them out, we redefine the object of the game as surviving and finding satisfactions in living. My bank robber analogy may be especially vivid if both members are in their second or third marriage, for battle-scarred couples, more conscious of their sense of guilt and desperation, can readily identify with the bungling pair who need help to redirect their efforts. Therapy for these couples must promote an atmosphere in which it is safer to claim disowned parts of the self than to continue to project them. As a therapeutic liaison evolves, the therapist can be delighted with any increasing acceptance of personal responsibility.

A frequent shared projective mechanism is the unholy bargain that goes as follows: "I have ambivalence and you have ambivalence that is painful to resolve. You take the top half of mine, and I'll take the bottom half of yours and we will fight like hell. That will feel better than the war inside."

— yuk

An example: He says, "She never wants to stay home." She says, "He never wants to go out." Choices and negotiation about staying home or going out require each person to deal with conflicts and desires within himself, bearing the responsibility of reaching decisions. It seems much simpler to define a cartoon, "You never want to go out"/"You never want to stay home," and fight.

Striking evidence of boundary problems between the members of a couple is the invasion of the other's internal self by assertive statements, "Of course you are angry at me—you've been that way for weeks. Go ahead and deny it; it doesn't make any difference because I know better." One of the classic and poignant tensions between people trying to be intimate is exhibited here. The speaker could be accurate! The partner has an unconscious and may, indeed, be repressing anger that the other picks up. Is one sensitive and the other repressing and oblivious, or is the other honest and one projecting? The tangle cannot be unsnarled by efforts to arrive at certainty and absolute answers. More often, the invasive statements go unchallenged and boundaries between the two become progressively muddled, until neither person can be clear about what he or she really feels or thinks. The result is isolation or murky border skirmishes, with each taking whatever position seems to offer a momentary advantage.

A particularly damaging kind of invasiveness involves the attribution of motives to the other partner. Of course, with troubled couples the assumed motives are usually ugly ones. Nowhere does the mechanism of the self-fulfilling prophecy work better than when frustration and disappointment are attributed to the other's wish to thwart and cause pain. Lacking external evidence, the accused cannot with certainty disagree. (For example, if a patient tells me that I want to embarrass him, not cure him, can I be sure that he is wrong? All I can say honestly is that I am unaware of any malignant attempt.)

Since invasiveness has so many bad results, it would seem that everyone would avoid it or resist it whenever possible, but this unfortunately is not so. A peculiar form of boundary problem is the insistence on invasive mind-reading as evidence of love and caring. "He should have known I didn't want to go; I just said I did to be agreeable." "She should have known I wanted to be alone," "He doesn't love me, I know; I always have to tell him what I want for Christmas or birthdays." Very small children must depend on the near mind reading quality of a mother's awareness of their needs. As they grow and develop speech, the responsibility for communicating needs moves to the developing self. But for many people, the real evidence of love would be a recreation of that early relationship when wishes seemed so powerful that speech was unnecessary.

This desire for mind reading can be sharply distinguished from empathic involvement. Members of healthy families regularly appear most empathic with one another, and yet they do not depend on this capacity. They are also open in communicating feelings, developing empathic understanding as they express who they are. Family members who have little empathic involvement with each other depend on mind reading and fear open communication.

Scapegoating is another form of projection, avoiding the recognition of internal conflict by blurring the boundaries between family members. Though the mechanism is the same as projection onto a partner, the resulting system shapes up quite differently. Instead of a bickering, mutually attacking pair, one sees a pleasantly cooperative couple wringing their hands over a third family member's obstinacy and impossible behavior. Ambivalence is handled not by recognition and resolution, but by projecting antisocial (antifamily) feelings onto a "chosen" child. This maneuver has superficial advantages; the spouses finesse problems between them, and the other children can play out warm and loving roles while using the scapegoat. (With more than one child, there will necessarily be at least one "Goody Two Shoes" to contrast with the scapegoated "Peck's Bad Boy") (5).

Overt Power Considerations

A definition is in order. *Power* has many different connotations, but is here defined to mean *the possession of control over or influence upon others*. This controlling influence can be expressed overtly or covertly, but overt power is a more trustworthy source of therapeutic comment since it is directly observable. In a family, or perhaps any group of people who define themselves as caring for one another, it is a defensible thesis that any person in the group has as much overall power as any other. A sick infant can control the activities of the whole family. A schizophrenic adolescent can bankrupt a father, cause siblings to be ignored, even split up parents, while remaining overtly helpless. A submissive wife, apparently disdained and thoroughly intimidated, can manipulate, control and influence much family activity. Therefore, I suggest that therapists carefully observe overt power differences in a couple. When the overt power is muddled, or when there is extreme disparity in its distribution, family rules are very likely to include many covert and illicit operations.

The pursuit of emotional health and personal enjoyment by couples involves *intimacy*—the joy of being known and accepted by another who is loved. There is no intimacy except when there is equal overt power! This idea can be supported both logically and empirically. If one is superior to another in station and authority, he or she must not express such leveling human feelings as fear, loneliness, wistfulness, uncertainty. Conversely, if a person is inferior to another, he or she must not show certain human characteristics that would be "uppity," such as assertiveness, a desire for respect, potent anger. Only when two people approach each other with the assumption of equality can they hope to know and be known by each other.

An adult who wishes to share a close moment with a child will make an effort to become physically eye-to-eye with the child. An all-powerful potentate can obtain sex and services from a slave without giving up that power edge, but if trust and love are desired the trappings of power must be abdicated, allowing the two to come together as equals. Partners in trouble have never recognized this correlation between equality and intimacy. They attempt to intimidate in order to find satisfaction; however, intimidation is only effective as it results in a power difference, so the possibilities of intimacy go out the window.

Intimidation can be overt or covert, direct or by the induction of guilt (which requires a kind of referee system). In overt intimidation, there are gross maneuvers, for example, "If you don't put your family money in our joint account, I will divorce you," as well as such subtleties as a slight hardening of the voice when unacceptable thoughts are expressed by the other. Overt intimidation through guilt induction can be dramatic, (''What would your father think if he knew how you treat your own child?'') or mild (''You didn't think to bring a present to your kids?''). Covert intimidation develops from a position of relative helplessness and may take the form of threats of illness: ''If you don't get your mother away from me, I'll go crazy again.'' Or the helpless partner may induce guilt, assuming the martyr's position: ''Yes, I put you through school, but you can divorce me now that you don't need me.'' None of these methods of intimidation to obtain a power edge will work between equals.

One can have unequal overt power with symmetrical roles (expected behavior patterns that are the same, e.g., both parents defining themselves as responsible for controlling the children) and there is a way to resolve conflict— the dominant person calls the shots. But in relationships with equal overt power, constant conflict is averted only by developing complementary roles: ''In this area you are the expert or the more responsible one and I will contribute as I can; in that area I am the expert or the more responsible one, and I will need you to help.'' Many couples who are currently in treatment develop impasses as the wife, tired of submissiveness in a conventional marriage, tries to reach for symmetrical equality with resultant non-negotiable conflict.

Case Example. An airline pilot and his wife had their first child rather late in their marriage. She had previously pursued a career and expressed great ambivalence about the housewife role. They agreed that each should spend the same amount of time with the baby. Interminable wrangles developed over who was to do what and when, who was shirking, etc. Finally they agreed to sort out and accept areas of primary responsibility for the child's care and other aspects of their lives. Each in turn was then able to take initiative and look to the other for help in roles which had become complementary.

Any viable system develops a leading edge; even in an amoeba, part of that blob transmits orders to and receives input from the rest. Parents functioning in complementary fashion must direct, control and influence children for that family to thrive. In competent families, the power differential diminishes over time as the children develop autonomy. As the children move through adolescence, parents can delegate authority and responsibility to them, functioning more as consultants or directors than as the powerful parents of small children. Finally the children become adults and speak with authority on their own choices and directions.

Though this pattern evolves in competent families and will avert the mythological beast of adolescent turmoil, most couples who enter treatment have attempted to use intimidation to control their children as well as each other. The therapist often needs to help the couples parent better by attending to these power issues. Learning to choose—to resolve ambivalence and move forcefully in a desired direction—requires the opportunity to make mistakes—to have the necessary overt power that goes with being responsible. In my experience, the parents of disturbed adolescents are woefully unaware of this technical reality and attempt to mold responsible adults by developing family systems where no one is responsible, hence everyone feels controlled by others.

Such a family continues, to a greater or lesser degree, the first interpersonal relationship that every person who survives infancy has experienced—the impotent/omnipotent mother/infant pattern. During this stage of relating, each is helpless and each is all powerful *at the same time*. Mother has the power of life and death over the infant; yet if the infant cries, mother may lose sleep, warmth and sex because of that cry. Child development can be usefully conceptualized as moving from this impotent/omnipotent way of functioning toward a sense of *competence*, from which total power and total helplessness are relinquished. One can have *relative* power through developing personal skills, but never absolute control with its flip-sided impotence.

In the disturbed family, boundary problems and overt power struggles thwart this normal developmental movement. One can see parents who feel as helpless as an infant (or its mother) regarding an adolescent son or daughter; yet at the same time that adolescent feels outmanned and outgunned, as controlled as an infant. Indeed, every sort of emotional illness can be seen to perpetuate this impotent/omnipotent relationship style. Fix it and you fix the ailment; do nothing about this interactional arrangement and therapy is interminable. Emotionally healthy people have confidence in personal power, but know it is always relative. Each of us must depend upon the warmth and living skills of others in order to trust our own competence.

During our research with both healthy and disturbed families, it became apparent that although raters could determine with good reliability the *style* of overt power in the family, they could not agree on *who* had that power. If forced to name the most powerful individual, the family became a Rorschach for the rater, who drew on his or her own family memories. If Dad was remembered as a strong and silent, the silent member would be defined as in control; if Mom was thought to be gabby and powerful, the talkative parent would be labeled as in power. From this we learned that overt power differences are balanced by covert illicit power and the presumed dominant person is as much trapped and controlled as the apparently submissive victim. Both are stuck in a rigid system that allows little negotiation or individual expression.

If individual emotional illness, like family and couple illness, is defined as stereotyped, repetitive, rigid, inflexible behavior patterns, then the whole family system must change if one person is able to increase his own autonomy and to proceed with successful individuation. Conversely, a deceptively simple way to define family therapy is to be oneself while in that family (25). If I can do that and not be pushed around, redefined or discounted, the family system has necessarily changed.

Control, Choice and Negotiation

When couples are encouraged to become autonomous and competent, both partners often fear that someone will suffer. Reaching for what one wants will be ugly, exploitative, selfish and—horror of horrors—controlling. Yet the wish to control others is ever present; to consider control efforts bad is to condemn people to neurotic guilt. Members of disturbed families usually get moralistic about control, and so do many therapists.

Among people wishing to be close, control is benign and valuable when it takes into account the choice of the involved individuals. In distant relationships, control of another with little concern for the other's choice may be quite reasonable and useful. Control issues are best handled, then, by a practical approach, acknowledging the human desire to control that part of the environment seen as needed. Starting from that premise, one need only focus on the wishes and choices of the people involved in a transaction to make it potentially close, warm, and an example of caring negotiation.

Where choice is ignored, a variety of covert behavior patterns develop which are interpersonal precursors to emotional illness. If, for example, family rules require that loving be shown by thinking and feeling just alike, the family suffers a dangerous double bind. One can express oneself and be defined as unloving and alone, or one can belong and feel loved but without choice. In such a family, children may develop choice by isolating themselves and engaging

enmeshment vs. disengagement
togetherness vs. alone

in a quiet rebellion that leaves them feeling guilty about the wish to be themselves. One sees two members collude, for example, an illicit mother/child relationship that undercuts father's efforts at control. Such patterns produce distance in the marital pair and shared guilt between parents and children. Incest, as well as many forms of behavioral disorders, requires this conscious or unconscious illicit collusion of family members who find it impossible to have needs met through the overt power structure. Individual problems are family system problems, and poor family rules usually are reflected in a tattered parental coalition.

Sex Stereotypes

Male and female stereotypes are rooted in overt power differences, and labels such as "compulsive" and "hysterical" cannot be understood without taking these power issues into account. Our family research found that those particular families termed "midrange centripetal" are the most predictable in developing children who show the classical cultural sexual stereotypes (5). Further information about this family assessment schema will be found in Chapter 6; we will just touch on the relevant material here. Stoic males, oriented toward control and with little access to feelings, are balanced by seductive, childlike females who never confront others openly but have a variety of manipulative techniques. The midrange centripetal family rules assume overt power differences and define whether children are to possess overt interpersonal power according to their sex. By contrast, "midrange centrifugal" families also believe in overt power differences according to the usual sexual stereotypes but cannot and do not carry them out. Father feels inadequate, gets drunk, leaves jobs, and blames his family for his difficulties. Mother resents being at home, feels her children are a burden, and desires to compete with men in confronting danger and seeking excitement. They both feel guilty over their "defects," verbally passing on to their children the same male/female standards and the same sense of guilt over not being able to live up to them.

Severely disturbed families and healthy families are relatively free of the sexist role definitions that make for dominant/submissive relationships involving proper Roman centurions and irrational lovable homebodies. The severely disturbed families are less entrapped in these stereotypes because they feel and are deviant; that is, they have no hope or expectation of being model families or of being accepted by the broader community. Overt power is usually unclear, and important decisions are reached covertly and illicitly, without discussion or direct intimidation. Mother is as likely to have power as father.

Members of optimal families, on the other hand, have had experiences that encouraged autonomy and individuation. Hence, they can develop secure sexual identities without depending on current cultural models. In these families, birth order rather than sex seems to be the most powerful determinant in evolving character structure (5). The oldest child, whether male or female, tends to be more concerned about duty, somewhat isolated from his inner feelings, and a bit less sensitive, aware and loving than the youngest or the middle child.

The couples therapist must develop an atmosphere in which women can be open, assertive or even directly angry, and men can be tender, openly frightened or uncertain. During treatment of midrange couples, as the personal repertoires of both spouses expand, one usually witnesses a transient reversal, with the woman becoming a strident harpy and the man exhibiting a frightened passivity. It is important to know that this reversal is temporary and to distinguish this kind of oscillation from growth. A Punch and Judy show is still stereotyped, whether Punch hits Judy or vice versa. When a female who has previously attempted to play a stereotyped "hysteric" role first tries assertiveness, she will become aggressive and hostile as well, since her self-image is still that of a little person. With a little experience she will learn that she can drive away the very person she hungers for, since men are also needful and vulnerable and have limits. Similarly, the "compulsive" man who is power oriented and unaware of feelings requires a little time to realize that women, like himself, need to have confidence and substance in order to be lovable and trustworthy. He learns to respect her thoughts and wishes, not out of duty or responsibility, but as a practical means of getting his own needs met. That gaining satisfaction is intimately related to giving satisfaction is one of the many paradoxes of human existence.

Contextual and Contractual Clarity

Insanity is a disease of context. A firm expectation of clarity of context is a bid for sanity. Hazy, ambiguous agreements (who is supposed to do what, what roles each will play, what is the point of their involvement) produce painful, crazy, messy dilemmas. The healthy family provides contextual clarity for members with clear expectations and promises. These family members also understand that to choose one role requires renouncing many other possible or fantasied roles ("if you are my mother, you are not a girlfriend"; "if you are my father, I must find someone else to be my lover"). One of the attractions of crazy relationships is that they deny or attempt to finesse these limits. ("I am your mother, but perhaps we can also be lovers in shared fantasy so long as neither of us acknowledges the desire or the conspiracy.")

Case Example. Mr. A., a handsome 42-year-old engineer recently separated from his wife, decided to try a reconciliation and invited his wife to come to sessions with him. He complained that she wasn't honest with him, that he never knew where he stood. Their daughter, age 20, had come home from college, and during the therapy session Mrs. A. expressed some open anger over a triangular incident of the previous evening: ''You fawned all over her. You not only ignored me, but chewed me out for expecting her to rescue her own burning dinner. You even told me to do it myself. You treated me like a servant.''

He responded, ''You mean I can't even talk to my daughter without your getting angry?''

''Well, you asked her to go out for dinner and dancing and you haven't asked me to do that in over a year.''

Even with this overt romantic invitation acknowledged, Mr. A. found it difficult to understand that his behavior toward his wife and daughter contributed to contextual confusion for all parties. Mrs. A. had an equally difficult time recognizing that her abdication of the sexual, lover role had contributed to the triangular confusion.

Though ambivalence is ubiquitous, the resolution of ambivalence is possible and necessary for contextual clarity. Mr. A. desired his wife, had romantic feelings about his daughter, and also experienced longing for a girlfriend he had dated while separated. He was disappointed and angry with his wife, had normal horrors of incestuous feelings toward his daughter, and was quite fearful that the attraction to his girlfriend was only sexual and therefore doomed. Mrs A., though consciously longing for her husband's return, had a lingering resentment over his handling of her substantial financial resources and frequently attacked him about this. She also compared him unfavorably to her father, whom she had continued to romanticize.

Mr. and Mrs. A., in order to become more competent, coherent and trustworthy with one another, required an increased awareness of their mixed feelings and the necessity to resolve them. By making such decisions, partners can accept the frustration of a finite, limited life that provides real satisfactions, even though these are inevitably less than the fantasied satisfactions of an ideal life or partner. Each individual then experiences tension within, rather than battles with the spouse. Each can see the other as a friend dealing with similar tensions, rather than as an enemy thwarting one's aspirations and goals. Clarity of context in the family system goes hand in hand with individual resolution of ambivalence and the responsible expression of choice.

To wean people from the dubious advantages of murky context, to understand powerful resistances to change, and to teach communication skills effectively, the therapist must recognize the covert power of fantasy. Many perceptive writers, such as Ibsen (*The Wild Duck*) and Miller (*Death of a Salesman*), have dramatically illustrated the importance of illusion in lives threatened by despair. To such individuals, clarity of context and coherence are a dreaded risk. In healthy families, communicational skills are both a cause and a *result* of successes in being a limited person who loves in spite of the other's acknowledged limits. Being personally responsible for feelings, thoughts, and behavior, being open to others and respectful of their unique feelings and perceptions, being vulnerable and clear—all help create intimacy and reduce unrealizable fantasies. A couples therapist who wishes to teach such skills must create a climate that rewards commitment, clarity, and the acceptance of personal ambivalence and limits.

Family of Origin

Family of origin issues are central to the discussion of context and contracts. The confusion of the past family with the present is a prime cause of spouses' feelings of betrayal, accumulated resentments, and vicious attacks, as well as a major deterrent to compassion and understanding. The two outstanding characteristics of problems with one's family of origin are *nonselective repetition of the past* and the ignoring or *distorting of data in the present*. More simply, there are problems with the here-and-now and problems with feeling small in relation to others seen as big.

Though each person's memories of family are unique, the common thread involves feeling small, like a child in comparison to the parent. This is the wellspring of fear that can produce intimidation, meanness of spirit and lack of compassion. Both members of a troubled couple often feel small; each sees the other as more powerful, more parental, and relatively invulnerable. Recreating the family of origin scenario in the present, with each member expecting and fearing that the other will be a good parent, leads each to feel betrayed, since each believes good parents give what the child needs. I find that the phrase "She (or he) could if she (or he) would" captures this regularly found pattern of transference, while "she (or he) would if she (or he) could" describes the direction the couple must go in order to find contentment. If I see my lover or spouse as parental, well nigh omnipotent, then I see myself as a hungry child, little and impotent. Any frustration will then be interpreted as a result of the other's malevolent intent, justifying the use of any and every control method available. I can intimidate, browbeat, or induce guilt without guilt of my own or even without compassion, since my lover is my adversary.

A therapist can work with these residuals from the family of origin as shared projective phenomena, encouraging a here-and-now orientation. Seeing partners together provides a natural exhibition of the split-off parts of oneself, similar to a Gestaltist "chair technique," where a person speaks to a denied part of himself in an empty chair and then moves to that chair and speaks in response. It is more complex, of course, with a live person in the chair who is also doing a bit of distorting and projecting but who can speak for him or herself.

An interesting projection pattern often seen in couples is a split projection, with the partner seen as powerful and parental and at the same time as childish and irresponsible. Each partner sees the other as a mean and foolish enemy who yet must be convinced of one's own value. Such an effort is like a grudge tennis match played with the opponent defined as line judge. As these two contradictory perceptions of the partner are brought to awareness, a breakthrough can occur as distortion and interfering memories are openly acknowledged for the first time.

Relationship Possibilities and Relationship Rules

In couples therapy it is helpful to consider the many relationship possibilities in a human life and how the rules for success vary in these different relationships. I find that many people are quite confused about such matters and often feel they should obey the same rules for relating to lovers and acquaintances, friends and business associates.

Imagine a person placed in the center of his or her universe, with concentric circles moving outward. The inner circle represents those few intimates that humans have, the next represents close friends, and following that, acquaintances, employees, employers, and so on out to people such as ticket takers or ushers in theaters. Placing people in each of these categories is a personal activity requiring both the resolution of ambivalence (and therefore choice) and the recognition of environmental possibilities (that is, the other's agreement to be in that particular circle). The rules of these different relationships vary greatly depending on the degree of closeness.

To succeed in intimate relationships, one must be reasonably open and honest, have equal power, and resolve rather than ignore differences. These same rules, however, would be woefully misguided in a peripheral relationship, for example, between an executive and one of 25 junior clerks. Partners who understand the varied degrees of closeness and the skills required to develop context clarity in different kinds of relationships can make clear contracts that encourage trust.

Sane but limited people who come from control oriented families often reverse the rules of close and distant relationships. With peripheral people they may offer elaborate respect and an effort at egalitarianism, reducing power differences that might be threatening to the interaction. On the other hand, these same people will treat spouses, children and parents with contempt, browbeating and intimidating without a qualm. Gentleness, shared dignity and mutual respect disappear when family members come home. As I speak of these circles and the rules for each, troubled partners can conceptualize their task as learning context and relationship rules and skills, a much more encouraging prospect than believing that one must change either the partner's personality or one's own in order to feel better.

Love and Trust; Warmth and Negotiation

Everyone wants the love of others; however, the definitions of love are extremely varied. To offspring of severely disturbed families, it often means finding someone who will be the embodiment of one's fantasies; these same people usually try to express love the same way. The toughest antisocial characters (''sociopaths'') of my experience have invariably had histories of short periods of trying to bend themselves into the shape of someone else's dreams, only to become enraged by the poor returns of such an effort.

Many sane-but-limited people define loving as wishing for and appreciating control. Love is imagined to be pure, unsullied by ambivalence or anger, often with the related belief that love is selfless, with selfishness the polar opposite of love. "He doesn't love me," usually means something like, "He doesn't do what I think he should," or "He has needs of his own that he stubbornly pursues, and he seems uninterested in meeting my needs the way I would like." Trust is split off from love by these frustrated people; both partners in a couple profess their love for the other, with simultaneous accusations of lying, deception and untrustworthy behavior.

Case Example. Mr. W. rarely was at home when expected, nor would he call if delayed; he pursued a dream that if his wife loved him, he would not have to be predictable. Mrs. W. would at times turn on her husband and verbally cut him to shreds; she believed that to be worthy of her love, he would be adequate (in her eyes) with no help from her.

My definition of love is *caring about another's well-being almost as much as one cares about one's own.* It is important to emphasize from the start of any couples treatment the value of each partner's "selfishness." Only this orientation can encourage openness, recognition of ambivalence, the evolution of responsible choice, and the clarification of personal boundaries. In addition, promoting selfishness encourages relative trust, since people who are motivated by their own admitted self-interest are more predictable and less erratic, while those who operate from "shoulds" and "oughts" have a propensity for being nice and then attacking or withdrawing.

If each person is rigorously responsible for his or her own best interests, this will be rewarding and helpful to the partner. If one partner wholeheartedly does not want to live with a spouse, both are going to be miserable in tandem. If the partners decide to live together, either person's delight and joy will be gratifying or at least educational for the other. "No martyrs allowed" might be symbolically emblazoned on the wall over the hearth. In this environment, *warmth* can be developed. I define warmth as *human need, honestly expressed, with a recognition of the inevitable limits of the other.*

All three aspects of this definition must be attended. Need, not selflessness, is its source. A "cold" person acts as if the other is not desired or needed. To be hungered for is to experience warmth. Honest expression of needs may require much new learning. People who have been taught that human need is sinful, ugly, disgusting, weak, or humiliating use all sorts of gambits—obscuring, denying, intimidating, and sermonizing.

The third part of the definition—recognizing the limits of the other—also requires considerable skill. If one sees a partner as another hungry, lonely, vulnerable, ambivalent human, projections are minimized and one's own self-interest fosters compassion, empathy, and the desire to meet needs in the other. If a farmer wants milk, he takes great pains to feed and care for his cow. People will do no less for each other once the system-dictated reciprocal needs and potential rewards are understood.

Negotiation becomes the usual method of solving problems when boundaries are clear, overt power is equal, the context and expectations are clear, and enlightened selfishness is the guide for the relationship. *By necessity* each partner becomes almost as interested in the other's choice and needs as in his or her own. The rules of intimate relationships require this; there is no need for coercion from parents or others, remembered or current. Crises of development and of loss can be flexibly met.

SUMMARY

A systems approach to human problems always embraces multiple levels. In this chapter, I have attempted to talk first of concepts and issues important at the individual level—ambivalence, projection, child development, guilt, boundaries of the self, sexual identity—and then present important concepts at the family systems level—boundaries, power, control, sexual stereotypes, context and contracts, family of origin relationship possibilities and roles—with the goal of relating all these issues to love and trust, warmth and negotiating ability. If the separation appeared somewhat artificial and inadequate, so much the better, because system thinking is interactional not only at a given level, but also between levels of human experience. Individual ambivalence is isomorphic with family conflict, for example, and successful intervention will resolve ambivalence as it resolves conflict. Negotiation is a process of individuals utilizing system rules.

3 ATTRIBUTES OF THE HEALTHY COUPLE

Any treatment effort assumes that something is wrong and needs "fixing." Further, it assumes that the therapist not only recognizes things that are wrong, but also knows what is normal, functional, and effective. Relatively little has been written on the clinical study of healthy couples or healthy families, however. This is especially true if one considers data-based studies. There was the pioneering effort of Westley and Epstein in 1969 (49), followed by the Timberlawn research group's study published in 1976 (36). In addition, certain studies of family pathology utilized healthy control groups, which provided data and insight into healthy family processes (40,42,47).

A general consensus of these studies was that, in the intact family, the quality of the couple's relationship is a critical factor in the quality of family functioning. Westley and Epstein's finding that, in many healthy families, couples reported marital satisfaction, even though one or both showed marked defects when evaluated individually, beautifully illustrates that "the whole is greater than the sum of the parts."

In the Timberlawn study, the focus was on observable, enduring patterns of interaction that were related to individual psychological health and illness. Clues to thought patterns and attitudes associated with family competence were also provided. Contributing to and supplementing these years of research were many thousands of hours of clinical work with troubled individuals, couples and families.

The data from this coordinated effort has led me to develop strong convictions about definable systems variables associated with physical and emotional health in family members (5,6,9,13). Further, I believe these variables can be influenced by treatment—for good or ill.

Bergin's studies (14) of psychotherapy outcome warned therapists that psychotherapy was not ineffective, as detractors had maintained, but rather that, as a result of the therapeutic intervention, people got very much better or very much worse than controls. In other words, the therapeutic relationship is not insignificant; it is powerful, and yet, like radiation in the early days of x-rays, the power can be damaging as well as helpful. It is my belief that therapists who are sensitive to systems issues and understand systems variables associated with family and marital competence are much more trustworthy, that is, more likely to help rather than hurt in the treatment of couples.

This chapter is an attempt to describe patterns in couples who are successful in maintaining a relationship that is satisfying to both for many years, one that adapts well to the changes brought about by the progression of both individual and family life cycles. These patterns are divided into two groups for the sake of clarity: those evidenced by speech (that is, attitudes and beliefs) and those determined by immediately observable behavior (interaction patterns).

HEALTH-PROMOTING BELIEFS

The beliefs associated with health in couples include 1) relative rather than absolute truth, 2) subjective reality, 3) the basic neutrality or benignity of family members' motives, 4) human encounter as rewarding, 5) a systems point of view, and 6) value and meaning in the human enterprise. These health-promoting beliefs will be described and contrasted with beliefs of less fortunate couples.

Relative—Not Absolute—Truth and Subjective Reality

One of the most helpful beliefs successful couples have is that people are limited and finite and therefore never possess the unchallengeable truth. All human computing apparatus, though marvelous, is subject to error. Our perceptions, memories, logic, and conclusions are fallible; therefore, honest differences usually can become an opportunity for synthesis rather than a necessary indication for struggle.

In contrast, most dysfunctional marital partners believe that truth is absolute and knowable. With this point of view, if my perceptions, memory or conclusions are challenged, then my very being is being challenged, and I must conquer or be vanquished. This unfortunate belief leads to the fear of encounter and efforts to avoid conflict that would logically be unresolvable. Usually these certainties are derived from one's family or origin. A revered parent or a despised one can be the source of absolute truth; the revered one passes it on directly, the despised one offers such a negative absolute that the offspring believes anything to the contrary. In many areas, such as politics, religion, child-raising or family rules, families can pass on opinions that deny uncertainty and human limitations.

Healthy couples have an abiding uncertainty and seldom get into the dreary "did/didn't," "was/was not" struggles that punctuate dysfunctional marriages.

People as Basically Neutral or Benign

There is a close relationship between family and couple functioning and the shared belief that people close to you have decent motives. Individuals need not hold any global, philosophical belief in the goodness of man; in fact, healthy couples may believe that large portions of the world's population are of evil intent. They *do* need to believe in the potential trustworthiness of their own spouse, parents, and children.

This belief allows people to err and disagree without the threat of isolation or abandonment. Human frailty is not translated into evil and perversity. When husbands forget birthdays, when husband and wife argue about the wife's outside employment, when children utter obscenities, destroy a plant or torment a pet, believing in the basic badness of these people makes for reassuringly simple explanations but limits or damages the relationship.

Several satellite beliefs are necessary to support the concept of people's basic decency. One must assume that sexuality, anger, willfulness, and deep ambivalence are a part of the human condition—sometimes not good, but hardly evidence of intrinsic malevolence.

Ambivalence is worthy of special mention. I have rarely seen any respect for ambivalence in dysfunctional couples! "You don't love me" is a frequent response to the pain produced by a spouse. "Of course I love you; I was just (stupid, careless, drunk, absentminded)," is often the retort. It is both useful and reassuring to know that people are indeed ambivalent about anything that is finite and yet needed—such as loved ones, jobs, support systems. Ambivalence can be resolved but never eliminated. Healthy couples know this and tolerate outbursts of bad feelings from spouse and children without using such negative experiences to "prove" evil intent.

The contrary view of man's basic malevolence produces distancing between people and causes what I have termed the "war in the nursery," with parents defining their love by how much they control and discipline. Believing their job as parents is to beat out the basic willfulness of an evil child can also lead to child abuse, which is justified as the policy of loving parents.

Human Encounters Can Usually Be Rewarding

Combining a healthy respect for uncertainty with the belief that family members are not malevolent goes a long way towards developing a climate of trust and cooperation. If spouses can trust each other and cooperate reasonably well, their experiences will lead them to believe that human encounters are usually rewarding. That is, they have *optimism*, a mind-set that hard work can be effective when human situations are bad and that there is reason to hope even in miserable situations, such as when a spouse is not trustworthy or a child is alienated and hostile. Hope is essential to successful endeavor, and healthy couples have it. This biological given of the newborn (12) has been maintained by the experiences of these fortunate individuals.

A Systems Point of View

My experience with healthy couples confirms that they intuitively recognize and operate on what I have come to call a systems point of view. This view includes at least four basic assumptions:

a) Any individual needs a group, a human system for individual definition, coherence and satisfaction.
b) Causes and effects are interchangeable.
c) Any human behavior is a result of many variables rather than one single cause.
d) Since humans are limited and finite, a social role of absolute power or helplessness prohibits many of the needed satisfactions to be found in human encounters.

Healthy couples know that people do not prosper in a vacuum; human needs are satisfied in an interpersonal matrix. As a child develops and matures, he or she leaves one system—the family of origin—not for isolated independence, but for other human systems. Whether he or she enters college or marriage, the military or the swinging singles, this person will continue to need community and must develop interpersonal skills to adapt to the next system. Some theoretical concepts give short shrift to this reality (just as disturbed families do) and define maturity as hypothetical independence, something close to being alone. Healthy couples do not make this error, but rather define maturity as the evolution of new relationships which provide reciprocal satisfying intimacy. Adults develop skills in meeting the needs of others as well as their own. Humans are accepted as social animals that grow up, leave home, and necessarily establish new close relationships.

This awareness promotes an open system, one with rules compatible with (though not necessarily the same as) those found in the larger society. People with peculiar rules carried over from their family of origin find it harder to leave home and establish a new family.

The second quality of a systems view of the world—the recognition that causes and effects are interchangeable—is equally significant. Dysfunctional couples are awash in confusion, looking vainly for clear identifiable causes for their frustration and pain, and they often retreat to vague or mystical answers, such as fate or destiny, for explanations of personal and family problems. Other dysfunctional couples seek oversimplified causes for human problems, for example, a bad seed within the household (scapegoating) or human perversity (evil drives), and they flounder forever in their efforts to control these evils.

Healthy couples know that, for example, hostility in one person promotes deception in the other and deception promotes hostility. Efforts at tyrannical control increase the possibility of angry defiance, just as uncooperative defiance invites tyrannical control. Stimuli are responses, responses are stimuli, in a process with shape and form but with no clearly defined individual villains or victims.

The third assumption—that human behavior results from many variables—is a vivid awareness of healthy couples.

Dysfunctional couples often consider only one explanation for a human problem. An example may assist in elucidating this difference. A child of three spills milk at the table. There are a number of possible reasons why the milk is spilled. Perhaps it is accidental and no motive should be attached to the behavior; or perhaps it has the interpersonal meaning that the child has a personal score to settle with mother; or perhaps the child is angry about an incident unrelated to mother; or possibly the child is tired and anxious and therefore apt to make mistakes; or maybe the problem is a mechanical one—the glass is too large and little fists are unable to hold it. A dysfunctional couple will use one of these approaches almost exclusively, whatever the situation. Optimal families use all of these notions and more. They are not locked into stereotyped responses from theories of simple causation, and their responses to an event vary with the context in a highly pragmatic fashion.

Meaning to the Human Enterprise

A great deal of people's energy and sense of purpose is tied up in neurotic interaction. Freud once remarked that neurosis was a private religion (27); Berne, who simplified the psychoanalytic to tinkertoy proportions, spoke of "games people play" with the same implications (15). Fighting back from the insult of the night before can be a reason for getting up in the morning. Taking care of a depressed spouse can provide some meaning in existence.

But what do healthy (or successfully treated) couples do to provide reason to work, for making and keeping commitments, for continuing the various processes of being a successful human with a social network? The usual answer, caring about loved ones and supporting their needs, by itself can lead to dysfunctional family interaction rather than health. Parents are threatened by children's growth and development; children fear leaving home as each individual's identity is intertwined with that of other family members. Even the mutual support that healthy partners provide one another is not enough to sustain purpose.

Healthy marital partners also have meaning that transcends their own skin and the boundaries of their family members. It may be provided by conventional religion or by a passionate cause—perpetuation of the wilderness, protection of the environment, preservation of capitalism and the American way of life, or fighting nuclear proliferation. The content seems unimportant (at least to an observer), but having a belief that directs energy and provides community with others outside the family is vital.

With many couples it has been my happy experience to see, as old neurotic struggles and games are seen through and put aside, the emergence of new energy and power requiring direction. When this happens, an interest in a previously significant religious structure may be rekindled, or a cause that has been given lip service becomes actively supported, or entirely new sources of transcendent meaning are found and acted upon. Often both partners are active; sometimes one is more active and the other operates as supportive stabilizer. In either case the ideology is usually important to both.

OBSERVABLE PATTERNS

Observable patterns are, of course, not totally separate from shared attitudes. Attitudes are internal representations of interpersonal patterns—usually from the family of origin—and function to develop ongoing interpersonal behavior.

Conversely, one can often deduce attitudes from observed behavior. But observation is in many ways more trustworthy than reports of beliefs, and the congruence between the two is very important in determining the health of couples. The behavior patterns to be described include: 1) a modest overt power difference, 2) the capacity for clear boundaries, 3) operating mainly in the present, 4) respect for individual choice, 5) skill in negotiating, and 6) sharing positive feelings.

A Modest Overt Power Difference

Ideally, two people who choose to live together and make a partnership would have precisely equal overt power. That is, neither would be observed to use such power maneuvers as imperious hand signals, drowning out the other, or guilt induction to control the other. In real life, this ideal is rare, but healthy couples are on the low end of a scale of overt power differences. Most of the time these partners respect each other's perceptions; they are able to negotiate and occasionally fight without assuming a one-up/one-down position.

Only in situations of equal overt power can there be *intimacy*—the experience of being open, vulnerable, and able to share one's innermost feelings and thoughts. At any age, with anyone, overt power and intimacy are highly correlated. In relationships of unequal overt power, the top dog is fearful of exposing weakness. Conversely, the bottom dog is fearful that anger, assertiveness, wishes for equality or domination will surface. Therefore, each is necessarily isolated to a significant degree.

The sexual encounter is probably the best, most dramatic example of the relationship between power and intimacy. With equality, risk-taking and dialogue are possible. The twin threats to sexual satisfaction—spectatoring and performance anxiety—are minimized. The embrace, to be healing, must include equality of the partners. Otherwise, there is inevitably a loss of dignity and some reduction of humanness in the sexual act itself.

The sexual encounter also gives us a valuable example of *how* equal overt power can be developed and maintained through *complementarity*. This word is defined as "the interrelationship or the completion or perfection brought about by the interrelationship of one or more units supplementary, being depended upon, or standing in polar position to another unit or units" (Webster's Third New International Dictionary, 1971). This rather dry definition highlights the fact that complementarity can offer cooperation, joy, and effectiveness without subjugation or an overt power difference.

Such a finding is relevant to the broader social issues concerning the rights of women and the possible threats to males as women have attempted to become more powerful. Equal overt social power is beneficial, not damaging, if there are complementary rather than symmetrical role relationships. In both long and short time frames (months and years as well as minutes and hours), optimal couples demonstrate complementary roles—such as teacher and taught, speaker and listener, aggressive role definer and supportive partner, breadwinner and homemaker, volatile reactor and calm dampener. This complementarity allows from more equal overt power without hostile competition and rivalry. Complementary roles need not be stereotyped; they need not slavishly follow cultural expectations, but they must exist when overt power is equal in order that relating can be shared enjoyment rather than continual struggle.

Complementarity and role differentiation appear necessary to allow pleasant interaction with shared dignity. A metaphor for such a situation is a sport such as basketball: On unskilled teams everybody tries to get the ball and shoot baskets; on skilled teams, players cooperate with complementary roles. While some have used complementarity to mean an unequal power differential (48), this is not an accurate definition nor is it how the term is used here. Overt power is an important behavioral dimension of healthy couples; role definition with complementarity rather than symmetry is another.

Capacity for Clear Boundaries

Healthy couples are capable of telling the difference between one person's feelings and wishes and another's. This ability is extremely important in working together, in making decisions which are supported by both, and in being with the other and feeling good. I use the same model of optimal boundaries for families as for individuals—that of the living cell. The cell boundary has integrity; it is quite clear what is in and what is out, yet it is optimally permeable to the outside world, allowing effective interchange.

I have come to realize that the discarding of acknowledged boundaries is not what defines pathology in couples; nor is the stubborn insistence on maintaining boundaries an indication of health in the relationship. In the midst of passion—whether angry or ecstatic—boundaries are lost. Sometimes such merging is delightful; sometimes it is horrendous. Healthy couples experience this just as dysfunctional ones do. However, the fortunate marital pair can regroup, clear up the boundaries, and reestablish effective dialogue between two sovereign persons. For example, all couples of my acquaintance quarrel. Some do it openly, some covertly; some are loud, some quiet. But none do so with maintenance of clear boundaries! When feelings run high, there is a juicy jumble of claimed and projected present and past, childhood memories and old hurts, frustrated wishes and dreams. During this time one must not expect a great deal of "sense," that is, reasonable dialogue and clear boundaries. But when passion has cooled, healthy couples can redefine where each ends and the other begins, and a productive resolution becomes possible.

Operating Mainly in the Present

My working definition of transference and family of origin difficulties is the phase "now versus then." Most problems that plague individuals and couples have a rather large component of experiencing the world as it was in childhood, assuming it consists of people who are clones of those in early life, and interpreting present situations *as* the past, rather than *in the light of* the past.

Healthy couples have families too. And those families have had a powerful impact—creating specific attitudes, expectations, and ways of operating that make up individual personality. Much family humor consists of some awareness of this history. Sometimes with delight, sometimes wryly, we see ourselves, our spouses, and our children repeating patterns we knew as youngsters. We can trace threads of behavior for three, four, even five generations, and wonder at the continuing mysteries of the coming together of nature and nurture. The trick in dealing well with present life situations is to know as much about the past as one can, remember it as best as one can, and look on it as a guide and not a directive. Capable spouses can usually do this because they possess what the analytic literature has called an "observing ego"—the ability to watch oneself interact, to critique, and to experiment with new ways of achieving goals. Using the past as a guide rather than as a prophecy goes hand in hand with pragmatic success in marriage.

Spouses in disturbed marriages are also influenced by their families of origin, of course. They often remember their growing up less well, and are much more apt to assume a stance with their own parents of either continuing to operate as a child or making a radical, self-conscious break. Either position makes it much more difficult to work through early relationships and clearly see them as different and separate from that which one has with a spouse.

I have been most impressed at the comparative ease with which healthy couples relate to their own parents, incorporating them in some fashion into their present lives and deriving satisfaction from these parents in a way that seems to add to, rather than diminish, the pleasure in the spouse's company. A similar happy experience can be observed with many couples in the latter phases of treatment. Usually, as treatment progresses, these spouses reach out to their own parents, if alive, to establish something solid and understandable. If a parent is dead, there will be a hunger to talk—with spouse and therapist—of that parent and to resolve some painful mixed feelings.

An acceptance of generational continuity seems to be an intrinsic part of marital health. Some aspects of family do not change through time, and some need to be changed. A present marriage can be better than the one that preceded it. Hope for making a better now is based both on memories of "then" and on current experiences.

Respect for Individual Choice—Autonomy

Our society places a premium on behavioral manifestations of a personal sense of autonomy. The autonomous person knows what he or she feels and thinks, takes responsibility for personal behavior, and interacts with others with a reasonably clear notion of choices. Westley and Epstein stated, "Autonomy seems to be essential to the development of a satisfactory ego identity, for one must be permitted to consider oneself a separate person and to experience oneself as such, to find an identity. Without such autonomy, it seems unlikely that the child will be able to solve the basic problems of separation from his family of orientation and will remain overdependent" (49).

An effective way to observe the degree of autonomy present in a couple's relationship is to see how much respect there is for individual opinions and choices. Fortunate couples have evolved a system with rules that allow, even encourage, the identification and expression of personal perceptions and wishes. This is, of course, a necessary ingredient in successful negotiating. The qualities mentioned thus far are most important in encouraging choice. If a human system encompasses a modest overt power difference, the capacity for clear boundaries, and beliefs in the basic decency of the self and partner and in the inevitable subjectivity of any human truth, members can make decisions more easily and can resolve ambivalence instead of dithering or projecting.

Resolving one's mixed feelings and making choices are necessary contributions to a loving relationship. Healthy couples know this and generally operate this way. They can usually express to each other significant personal desires, fitting them to the limits of the situation and the people involved. For example, one healthy couple made the transition from conventional father/breadwinner, mother/housekeeper pattern to a system where both adults are working and the children grown up. The wife had been content with the husband's earning capacity, tailoring her wishes to the husband's income. As her work level decreased in the home, she began to want to work outside for more money and for what it could bring. The husband was able to take this transition in stride by defining what was most important to him, that is, her emotional support. Their negotiations made it possible to have what was most important to each.

These transitions often founder when people have difficulty resolving their own mixed feelings and are unable to define wishes and needs clearly. Spouses in dysfunctional marriages then fall back on intimidation, trying to fit themselves and their spouses to some kind of stereotype—long-suffering or outraged husband, liberated or subservient wife—and both feel cheated.

Skill in Negotiating

All of the attributes of a healthy couple come to fruition in the skill of negotiating problem solutions that meet both people's needs. The most rapid way to determine the health of a human system is to ask that system to do something. In our studies of families and couples, we have asked them to "plan something together," to "discuss the best and worst in your marriage," or to "decide what you would like to see changed in your family." Such tasks require negotiating, discussion, and resolution of differences; this negotiating ability along with positive feelings, is closely correlated with health (13). To see a healthy couple or family work on a task is a systems researcher's delight: Boundaries are clear, mixed feelings are resolved, caring is expressed, goals are defined and decisions are made.

Sharing Positive Feelings

The final observable quality of healthy couples is the sharing of positive feelings. When the work of living is kept current (with little dust swept under the rug), encounters are effective, optimistic, and fun. Most people enjoy what they do well, and relating to a spouse is no exception. The mixture of personal skills and good humor while dealing with the serious challenges of family's life cycle is most impressive.

SUMMARY

To summarize, the qualities of healthy couples found in formal research and clinical study begin with attitudes and thinking patterns, the most important being a benign view of one's own and the spouse's basic nature, and the awareness that human truth is always subjective. Behavioral characteristics include a modest overt power difference, the capacity for clear boundaries, focus on the present, and the capacity for making choices. These attributes culminate in skillful negotiating with good humor.

Section Two
ACUTE MARITAL CONFLICT

4 THE INITIAL INTERVIEW

When a couple enters a therapist's office, there is, as in any human encounter, a rich but confusing mixture of behavior and communication. All of us who intervene in people's difficulties practice reductionism. We achieve coherence by structuring reality; that is, we drop out some of the input that could overwhelm us and focus on that data which we believe will further our efforts within the context as we understand it. In so doing, we maintain hope of a satisfying outcome.

Though selecting and organizing are required of therapist and couple alike, there is one rather striking difference. Marital partners are demoralized. Their perceptions have not been sufficient, their strategies not adequate, to satisfy deeply felt needs. As they enter the therapist's office they half despair, half hope, that outside intervention can offer them more. In addition, most spouses have attempted to resolve problems by blaming each other and trying to intimidate one another into meeting unmet desires, persisting in these tactics despite their fruitlessness. Nevertheless, the very fact that these individuals come as a pair suggests their hope— for themselves, for the therapist's skills, and usually for the relationship (exceptions to this latter were discussed in Chapter 1). They bring a history of frustrating encounters, of clumsy attempts to ask or to give that have been misinterpreted or improperly decoded. At this point, most partners do not trust their own motives and may shout a lot about each other's deviousness. Further, they come from families of origin which have molded their expectations and patterns of behavior in close relationships; rarely does one speak with a troubled marital pair for long without hearing references to a spouse being "just like your mother" or "confusing me with your father."

THE HERE-AND-NOW INTERVIEW

In assessing individual patients, I am immediately eager to know not only the present situation, but also some information about where that person came from—the family circumstances, number and age of siblings, early memories and perceptions of parents. In a first interview with a couple, this is not such a compelling interest. The interactional material is more immediately important. There are several reasons for this greater focus on the present moment.

First is the urgency and emotional intensity in the couple's presentation. It would be a shame (and often a near impossibility) to block that feeling, to dam it up, unexpressed, while pursuing a meticulous formal history on each individual.

Second, the spouses' interactions with each other and the therapist offer a wealth of material eloquently dramatizing the past as well as the present. For example, a husband approaches his wife with a subservient, shamefaced quality appropriate to a grubby four-year-old whose live frog has just hopped from his pocket onto mother's white linen bedspread. Or a grown woman expresses to her spouse the impotent rage of a tiny girl who has been put to bed without supper. The therapist could launch an archeological exploration of relevant patterns from different layers of each personal history. The partners will, in time, put their wishes, fears, and behavior into an historical context, but first we need to confront the immediate feelings and hear how these people present the accompanying explanations.

③ Third, a capable therapist can, in the initial interview, provide a needed infusion of hope by offering something immediately useful in reducing conflict and giving each a greater sense of mastery in what they experience as a painful, confused mess. To do this he needs to observe patterns of interaction—systems data—and to bring that information to his patients' consciousness. I will discuss this much more later; the point to be stressed here is that immediate change does not come from insight into intrapsychic, family-developed phenomena, though this material may be quite useful in extended intervention.

THE DYAD

The initial contact made by one member of the pair is significant and may have a variety of meanings. Usually the person who calls the therapist is the one who feels most in pain. This may be because the partner is threatening separation or divorce, and the caller is desperately trying to find a solution other than dissolution of the marriage. (For convenience, I will refer to marriage in reference to couples; please add a mental asterisk, since bonds of cohabitation produce equal pain and satisfaction, and such couples now more frequently seek professional help.) It is useful to locate the obvious pressure for change, since this energy cannot readily be harnessed and directed.

"The Problem." There will be some stated reason for the two to appear together, and the therapist does well to attend not only to the content but also to the way it is presented and its implications of underlying beliefs and attitudes.

The problem may be expressed in starkly simple and concrete terms, "She doesn't like sex with me," or in vague generalities, "We are just incompatible." It can be described similarly be each person: She says, "He is so passive that it drives me crazy.'' He agrees, ''Yeah, she's right, I can't seem to be able to do anything about it.'' Or their descriptions may be wildly dissimilar and even the very statement of the problem produces a fight: He says, ''She is just terribly excitable, Doctor; if she could get her nerves under control we could have a happy marriage.'' She responds, ''Oh, it's still all me, is it? What about your ignoring me and the kids—you think that is easy to live with?''

Listening to the problem gives important clues as to the disturbed *process*. I define an individual neurosis as *stereotyped, repetitive attitudes and behavior that once were useful, even necessary, but now are inadequate, maladaptive and ungratifying*. Similarly, a couple's relationship disturbance consists of endlessly repeated stereotyped, simple interactions based on rigid, limited beliefs about the self and the partner which produce an unpleasant and painful relationship rather than a satisfying one. The way the partners present a problem will usually demonstrate for the therapist the way their disturbed interaction works. Identifying this simple pattern, and helping the couple become conscious of and alter it, constitute a most important aspect of treatment.

Nobody is all neurosis, and no couple interaction is entirely stereotyped. Helping the pair free themselves from a simplistic frustrating pattern allows them to be more varied, more ''human'' with each other. Strengths and possibilities in the relationship may also be evident when they state the presenting complaint. Some couples show a grudging respect or an obvious caring that mollifies their attacks and is expressed in puzzled, frustrated depression more often than in slashing anger.

To organize the information presented in the interview, I utilize the following categories: 1) power, 2) congruence of the self-report, 3) boundaries, 4) feeling expression, and 5) conflict resolution.

Relationship Power

Power here refers to overt power, the visible control capability demonstrated by the participants (4). It does not refer to covert control by apparent helplessness. Troubled couples may appear in such a tattered, fragmented state that neither partner attempts to gain control, but this is unusual, and when seen is accompanied by other signs suggesting severe individual emotional difficulty. Most of the time, one person attempts to have the overt power and the other either battles toe-to-toe to resist, submits sullenly, or, while ostensibly accepting the unequal power distribution, moves to covert control methods.

Since all of us have a fundamental need to signal others and obtain a desired response, that is, to *control*, it is axiomatic that the less the overt power, the more covert means will be used for needed control. The couple least able to share overt power will be caught up in an endless, frustrating struggle with no winners, or the partner who both agree is powerful will win every battle but feel overly responsible and emotionally deprived.

Congruence

Congruence of self-reporting refers to statements that each makes about himself, about the other, and about their situation. These may match well or poorly with the other's report, and each one's statements may be congruent or incongruent with the therapist's own perceptions of the couple.

Partners routinely disagree about the reason for the problem, usually blaming each other, but they often agree about their situation. "We have a crummy marriage," may be the only thing that a couple can agree on, and the therapist may wholeheartedly concur! In many troubled relationships, there

is a striking incongruence between the two partners' perceptions of the relationship. For example, one person may be
overwhelmed with frustrated hopelessness while the other
blandly minimizes the present difficulties, recalls good times,
and is ostentatiously oblivious to the other's despair. Personality characteristics are frequently sources of sharp dis-
agreement: "I am reasonable and you fly off the handle."
"You never want to have sex and I'm always ready." "I am
able to talk things out and you clam up." Such descriptions,
however unflattering, may be accepted by the other partner
but still not jibe with the behavior the therapist observes in
the treatment setting.

Case Example. The engineer and his graduate student wife (described in Chapter 1, see p. 13) evidenced this kind of incongruence between words and behavior, all the more jarring because
they agreed. In their initial interview the wife, in a tiny voice and
with many hesitant, incomplete sentences, dwelt on how aggressive she was, how she had to do everything, and how passive her
husband was. He agreed, even though it was he who had in-
vestigated marital therapy, made his choice of available sources,
and arranged for the appointment, as well as describing, in the
course of the history, several promotions and numerous patents
for which he was responsible.

Such disparity between the couple's shared reality and the
therapist's perceptions suggests that the two have blended family
myths reaching back to previous generations. The husband had
been carefully taught that sexual feelings and anger were evil,
hence found his wife's view of him reassuring, though unflattering, since it meant that his bad self was less likely to get out of
control. The wife had a strong wish to be aggressive and assertive, and her husband's acquiescence to her pretense bolstered
her shaky self-esteem.

Boundaries

Boundaries, the subjective borders between one person's
symbolic self and another's, are most important and will be

a major focus of our subsequent sections on treatment. Disturbed couples have boundary problems, and when these are resolved the individuals function better, whether separately, together, or with others. Boundary difficulties show themselves in the initial interview in, for example, "mind reading"—one partner insists that he or she knows what goes on inside the other and, if the other disagrees, responds with a knowing smile. Further illustrations include (depending on the level of sophistication): "You just don't want to admit it," or, "Of course you believe that," or, "What I'm referring to is unconscious." Sometimes a partner may *expect* mind-reading; one of the presenting complaints often is, "I have to ask for everything I get, and that spoils it. If she (or he) loved me, I wouldn't have to ask."

The most troublesome boundary problems involve projections, that is, ascribing denied attitudes of the self to the partner and attacking those qualities in the other person: "You never let me make decisions." "I know you don't love me, I don't care what you say." "If you would only stop being so angry—damn it!—we could enjoy each other." These boundary difficulties do not function independently but are shared between people who have lived together for years, each having made unspoken bargains with the other to allow this kind of reciprocal gross challenge to the integrity of the self.

Another shared phenomenon of troubled long-term relationships is avoidance of personal responsibility for feelings, thoughts and behavior by blaming, by appeal to an outside authority, by vagueness, by masking, by silent withdrawal, and by the complicated, confusing communications expressed in sarcasm, irony, and "humor" at the other's expense ("I was only joking"). Sometimes a couple may, with a shared kind of eerie humor, talk about terribly painful and ominous perceptions and experiences; my sensation is that of watching children playing cops and robbers with loaded revolvers. This peculiar method avoids responsibility, not by shifting or obscuring, but by denying the significance of these life experiences (as did the warring couple in Albee's *Who's Afraid of Virginia Woolf?*). It is important to ferret out any awareness of personal responsibility in undesired partner behavior. The beginning of a systems-oriented, competent relationship has its seeds in such an awareness. If each member of a couple can see any reciprocal involvement (for example, withdrawal leading to the other's sarcastic screaming fits, or screaming fits leading to the other's withdrawal), the engagement of each as a partner in the necessary change in made easier.

The reverse side of projection denial of responsibility is the equally maladaptive clutching of it. A depressed person often expresses a belief that she or he is responsible for a spouse's unemployment, a child's waywardness, or even a spate of bad luck. This extreme position is most effective in avoiding reasonable responsibility, as it invites others to insist that the person is really blameless—a complex ploy that requires others rather than oneself to put the blame elsewhere. Though this may not be the subjectively experienced motive, it often works.

Expression of Feelings

[handwritten margin note: 1) acceptable feelings? 2) prevailing feeling? 3) degree of empathy?]

Feeling expression includes several factors. First, how many feelings are expressable? A noisy couple may really be two Johnny-one-notes with, say, the wife subdued and wistful and the husband overtly angry, running the gamut of emotions from A to B. They carefully leave out lust, despair, tenderness, and fear, channeling all communications through the emotive expression that they have found least threatening, though perhaps quite painful.

In addition, the prevailing mood is significant. Is there some cautious optimism, some generosity of feeling? Does anger permeate the office? Or depression? Has despair promoted cynicism, with one outdoing the other in skillful thrusts and the proud refusal to acknowledge wounds? The severity of the problem will be closely monitored by this feeling tone.

A third aspect of feeling expression is the degree of empathy present. In spite of the conflict, the frustration, and the projection, are there moments when each senses and responds to an honest feeling in the other?

Conflict Resolution

It is clear that couples do not come into treatment if they have been able to resolve major conflicts well. However, in the course of one session, many small episodes of conflict occur which will be resolved, and careful observation is instructive. Who chooses the first chair? Patterns of assertiveness and submission are suggested. Who speaks first? Who describes the problem? When both speak at the same time, who relinquishes the floor, and how does that person appear? Does he or she show grace or is there a sullen, angry or resigned attitude?

How does the couple utilize the therapist in these small conflicts? Does one brazenly attempt to seduce the authority, inviting an ally? And does the spouse obligingly pick a fight, playing out the role of Peck's bad boy?

Resolutions of conflict can be of many sorts. Short-term resolutions depend on intimidation, seduction, submission. These can be quite effective, yet leave a tension in the relationship that is unresolved, heavy, and ominous. An even more slick but potentially dangerous resolution is *disengagement*: Both partners tacitly agree to ignore their own behavior and feelings. A little bit of this makes life bearable; extensive use derails needed negotiation.

These are factors relating to the pair's shared patterns. They probably relate also to each member's ability to express intimacy to anyone, but this is not necessarily so. It is possible that another person would make one or both of these people look much better in terms of both social skills and degree of satisfaction. This is the question troubled marital partners are usually trying to decide. Further, each partner must have an awareness of choice about living together in order to be content. The therapist will be most effective by teaching emotional awareness and assisting in individual growth; he will never "know" whether people should stay together or divorce. This ignorance provides the wisdom necessary to help people make choices for which they can and will claim responsibility.

INDIVIDUAL EVALUATION

A clinician needs the ability to assess current individual performance as well as a relationship. It is as important to arrange treatment for an acute psychosis or a severe depression, and not erroneously define the trouble *at that moment in time* as only a problem in relating, as it is to spot faulty systems and help individuals by improving their relationship patterns. Assuming the reader will have been trained in some system of evaluating individual functioning, I will not go into the methodology for such evaluation.

Even in a first session, some information regarding families of origin can help greatly in understanding individual world views, self-definitions and probable projections.

A few questions as to recent physical functioning are important. What are the sleep patterns for both? What drugs are being used, both prescribed and nonprescribed? There should be evidence of a recent physical examination for each partner. If such is not the case, referral to a family physician or internist is indicated. This is especially true for couples whose complaints are specifically sexual, but the procedure may also pick up physical problems that can masquerade as emotional illness, such as congestive heart failure, hyperthyroidism, drug-induced toxic states, malignancies, hypertension and the like.

Interaction With the Therapist

How do the partners relate to you? The skillful therapist will find transference or distorted perception most prevalent in the initial interview, decreasing from then on. Initially patients have the least information as to the specific qualities, beliefs and behavior patterns of the therapist, hence must depend on their fantasies and previous experiences with authority figures in anticipating what to expect and what is expected of them.

There is usually some variation on the theme of submission to, or defiance of, a judgmental, powerful figure. I have utilized the concept of "referee" to describe an inhuman, absolute power that is the rule-setter and judge of every family member's actions, thoughts and feelings. Akin to the familiar Freudian superego, this referee is shared by all family members (5). Few people who enter psychotherapy come from families where this phenomenon is not present. In troubled marriages, however, the referee system each member learned from his family of origin is used to intimidate the other by moralizing, shaming and blaming—methods that are powerful and painful but ineffective in producing desired change (1). As one indication, when the couple appears on the therapist's doorstep, at least one member (usually both) is hoping to enlist the therapist as an ally in a previously unsuccessful effort to intimidate and bring the other person into line with the mostly unconscious family referee. Often one or both partners are quite fearful that the judgment of the therapist will throw the power struggle into a hopelessly uneven match.

Case Example. Mr. and Mrs. M. came with the agreed-on complaint that the husband was drinking too much and, at sporadic intervals, spending evening hours in cheap bars with an odd assortment of male and female chance acquaintances. Both were sophisticated in the ways of therapy and therapists, and Mrs. M. initially evidenced a nonjudgmental and loving relationship to her husband as well as a trusting, nonmanipulating response to the therapist. Mr. M. told his rather shabby story with little obvious defensiveness, some candor, and a cool, nearly emotionless voice. In the second half of the interview, however, Mr. M. began to bristle at the therapist's questions, and as he became more challenging and defiant, Mrs. M. assumed her self-defined role as peacemaker between therapist and husband.

Mr. M. was the guilt-ridden son of a tyrannical, moralizing father. In his family or origin, he had at times tried, in a compulsive, dutiful fashion, to succeed; at other times he had been ostentatiously self-defeating and hostile. Mrs. M. was the oldest of seven children. Her memories of home were centered around taking care of younger siblings to help her overwhelmed mother. Their earlier patterns of attitude and behavior were played out within a few minutes of therapy, in spite of the conscious efforts of these two knowledgeable people to be "reasonable."

Of significance in the first interview are similarities and differences between the patterns of response to the spouse and those to the therapist, since these most clearly reflect family-developed and unconsciously absorbed roles and expectations.

Case Example. Mr. and Mrs. K. came into the office at the insistence of Mrs. K., who behaved for all the world like a harassed mother complaining to a child psychiatrist about her rebellious, slightly retarded five-year-old son. Her response to the therapist was instantly positive and showed the clear expectation of an alliance, while she obviously despaired of her husband/son's ability to change. Mr. K., in contrast, related exactly the same way to the wife and the therapist—shamefaced, anxious, covertly defiant

and hostile, with an eye roving about the room seemingly searching for a possible avenue of escape.

Mrs. K.'s mother had been depressed and intermittently psychotic throughout her childhood. Since her mother had been
unable to attend her needs, she judged herself to be unlovable;
she also felt justified in her unhappiness, as she had spent many
hours complaining to her father and being reassured and supported about her mother's transgressions.

The husband had grown up as the overindulged but emotionally deprived son of a wealthy father and a depressed, overcontrol-
ling mother. He grew up believing that he was selfish and insensitive but would nevertheless always be loved and pampered. His
guilt and defiance were long-term attributes. Once again, in a few
minutes, the observable threesome interaction gave powerful clues
as to specific family roles and expectations.

The therapist's feelings are most helpful in assessing the
relationship, for he or she is invited, often seduced, and occasionally bludgeoned to choose sides with the shared scenario of one oppressed/one tyrant. When I experience this
trend, I reflexly begin to feel "had" by both partners. These
couples almost inevitably conspire to involve the therapist
in their endless morality plays; a healthy appreciation for
the systems concept of circular causality offers needed strength
to resist their seduction.

Case Example. Mr. and Mrs. Z., a self-employed businessman and
his wife who worked in his business, came in on her initiative and
spilled out a story of his cruelty and insensitivity so dramatic as
to be hard to believe. She was warm-hearted, sensible, aware and
struggling; he was mean-spirited, cynical, proudly selfish, and
contemptuous of wife, children, psychotherapy in general, and
the therapist in particular. The husband's behavior and words
confirmed every bit of this story. In a few minutes my wish to
rescue her and kill him triggered my automatic warning buzzer,
but there was a nagging and irritating question: Why the collusion? I have seen a "Christian martyr" many times before, with

that stereotype's obvious advantage of avoiding responsibility and having others attempt rescue, but never had I seen such a whole-hearted and enthusiastic agreement by the partner that he was indeed the very embodiment of immorality and evil.

Mr. Z. remembered feeling ridiculed, impotent, frightened, and unloved by peers. His father was passive and withdrawn, and his mother, in a devastatingly confusing fashion, reassured him that he was lovable but also criticized him, often using the same character indictments that he heard from his playmates. He grew to adulthood believing that no one would ever love him, so he learned to intimidate them. Denying the fear, he became frighten-ing. To be attacked was to be somebody; not to be attacked was to be nobody.

In the heat of triangular interaction, the possibilities of openly expressed "countertransference" multiply, and it behooves every therapist to guard against responses manipulated and milked from him by skilled thespians who regularly practice their act.

SPIN-OUTS AND SPIN-INS

Interaction in disturbed couples is always organized in a particular pattern that leads to pain, grief, and hopeless-ness. One sees a stereotyped dance, choreographed with precision and performed in misery. A particular defensive pattern in her will trigger a particular response in him which produces a greater amount of her typical pattern, which leads to . . . and so on. If we call one partner's stereotyped maladaptive pattern "A," the other pattern "B," then A leads to B, which leads to more A, which leads to more B. I called this sequence, which is inevitable in troubled cou-ples, a *spin-out*. A therapist who can spot such predictable patterns within the first evaluative session and bring the couple's attention to it offers a valuable source of hope for the demoralized pair.

Several attributes of the spin-out require elaboration. First, this is a system diagnosis. It is more accurate than individual

spin outs

character diagnoses, since couples have a remarkable way, in this repetitive pattern, of switching roles and taking on the style of the partner. For example, one might describe a couple as a hysteric/compulsive match, with the wife being so dramatic and intense in her emoting that the husband becomes affectively withdrawn and super-rational. But six weeks later, he will come in loudly attacking and frightfully emotive, and she will show the withdrawn, superior, rational response. The spin-out pattern is the same, but conventional character-diagnostic concepts would be confusing. Whether Punch hits Judy and Judy provocatively runs or vice-versa, it is still a Punch and Judy show, and most couples will be found to be switch-hitters, capable of playing either role in the futile, frustrating struggle.

Second, the therapist's observation and delineation of a spin-out pattern require only close attention to the data of the interaction, rather than elaborate explanation of theory. Hence, it is a low-level interpretive effort as compared to more abstract interpretations regarding projections, family of origin repetition and the like. In the initial phases of work with a couple, therapist intervention at a low level of inference requires less trust. A better alliance, as well as more shared experience and assumptions, is required to make abstract interpretations coherent, meaningful and acceptable.

Third, calling the pattern to the attention of the struggling pair invites them to begin to think in a systems fashion, that is, to become aware that causes are effects and effects are causes, that one partner can influence the other's behavior though he cannot directly control it. Each person can experience his limited, finite, but real power rather than the impotence that is felt with omnipotent control efforts.

Case Example. In treatment Mr. and Mrs. K., the couple referred to earlier (p. 98) who caricatured the frustrated, controlling mother and the shamefaced, bad, little kid, became aware of how their pattern resulted in helplessness, anger, distancing and hopelessness. Mrs. K. realized that she had a good deal to do with his defensive, sullen, pseudo-apologetic posture, and Mr. K. realized that he triggered her exasperated, hostile attacks. Each had some control over what he or she did not want in the other person. (Incidentally, they did show the reversal of this pattern while in treatment, with Mr. K. attacking moralistically and Mrs. K. becoming defensively shamefaced. In fact, they alternated several times in the roles but not in the pattern.)

spin-ins

This leads to a final point about spin-outs. When they are recognized by the partners and made conscious, they can become *spin-ins*: Less A leads to less B, which leads to less . . . etc. As either partner reduces his contribution to the self-repetitive pattern, the other's response is reduced also, with the probability of greater closeness and sharing. Reducing or eliminating the shared neurotic pattern increases each person's confidence, competence, and adaptive skills, with dramatic improvement in the relationship.

Making these initial comments about the couple's behavior, the therapist interested in helping each partner develop relationship skills will take pains to be heard as a technician, not as a judge or moralizer. This is not the only method of couples therapy, but it is the approach taken throughout this book. Treatment of emotional illness by any strategy, whether individual, couple, family or group, can be divided into two categories: grower or controller. Both are respectable and both can provide some relief, but I believe the growth-oriented style is superior in increasing partners' living skills and thus reducing the likelihood of their return with new symptoms and no idea how to deal with them on their own.

INTERVENTION

Another vital aspect of the initial interview is the couple's responses to efforts at intervention. Treatment and evaluation go hand in hand, and the couple can have a generous sample of the therapist's wares at the first visit. As a spin-out pattern emerges, intervention can be made with respect for the data and the couple. A low-level inference can honor and illustrate the subjective quality of each participant's position, including that of the therapist. My effort is always to attend to my own choices as much as to the patients', to maintain my own dignity and personal boundaries, and to respect the same in patients. I have no desire to intimidate. The therapeutic effort is always toward increasing respect for personal choices, feelings and perceptions.

As observations are made tentatively, with appeal to shared or shareable information, some patients will quickly become reassured and reduce their own efforts at intimidation and control. These couples are a delight to deal with; their past histories have included some experiences of being treated with dignity, and so it is not entirely new territory for them. Other patients will pick up this orientation more slowly, with one perhaps becoming more open to discussion and exploration and the other redoubling efforts to enlist the therapist as a partner in coercion. Still others will be so caught up in the despair and struggle that respectful, gentle, and nondramatic interventive efforts are not effective. In such situations, more therapist emotion and expressiveness may be called into play; however, the point is always to evaluate the response and start a healing feedback loop.

This continuing role of the therapist as forceful but not intimidating, subjective but respectful of others' perceptions, I characterize as being a technician. Many years ago Erich Fromm made a distinction between being authoritative and authoritarian (28). The therapist must be knowledgeable about human behavior, but has no right to impose opinions on frightened, confused people.

My analogy for this posture is the architect. If people select an architect well, he or she will be technically proficient and even artistic, but these attributes provide no knowledge of what kind of building clients desire or need. This information must come from respectful dialogue.

In *Psychotherapy and Growth*, I elaborated on the theme that the scientific method is ideally suited for working as a psychotherapist since it is the optimal ego-building approach. To respect the patient's desires, fantasies, and wishes, to present oneself as an expert offering technical help and assessing the probabilities of success in achieving goals, is to provide role-modeling for ego functioning. Attending inner feelings and practical pragmatic issues of methodology will encourage strength by minimizing the attitudes and perceptions which define the patient as smaller and weaker. The control oriented therapist appeals to authority, prescribes and directs. The growth oriented therapist observes and invites partnership. The technician approach provides more *useful* information about the couple and their interaction. Since it is noncoercive and allows more freedom, the behavior in response will be more "natural"—more like the patterns at home.

There is a story of a king in the Middle Ages who commissioned a court carpenter to build a prison for his political enemies that was too low for the prisoner to stand up, too narrow to sit down, and too short to lie down. The prisoner must *squinch*—sort of lying down, or sort of sitting, or sort of standing—and each person would find whatever position was most comfortable—or least uncomfortable. This story has become a paradigm of the human condition for me. Being monogamously married, having affairs, being separated, divorced, single, or living in a commune—all have their attractions and frustrating shortcomings, as do the innumerable styles found within each of those situations. A properly humble couples psychotherapist will attend to each person's stated choice and help the spouses achieve their goals, whether shared or separate. In this process, the ubiquitous ambivalence present in everyone about every situation, person, and context can be recognized and resolved, until it arises in another issue to be dealt with again. Ego functioning, in other words, is in large part the resolution of ambivalence, maximizing one's satisfaction in an imperfect world populated by stumbling, error-prone fellow humans.

Marriage is a prime arena for the expression of unresolved ambivalence, with transference and projection the chief methods used to avoid acceptance of human limits. Every attack on the partner, every "should" and "ought," or every effort at intimidation is a child's dream of obtaining satisfaction through omnipotent control. Working with couples can provide a marvelous vehicle for helping people accept boundaries, limits, and finiteness without despair by developing negotiation skills and increasing the awareness of shared hungers and shared dreams.

By the end of the first interview, a therapist will usually have some reasonably clear notion of why the partners came in, of the best and worst that they have been able to do in relating to each other, and of the shared, repetitive stereotyped pattern which defeats their efforts at intimacy. In addition, he or she will have made some attempts at intervention and will have learned how deeply mired the pair is in the muck of their efforts at control by intimidation.

The couple, in turn, will have learned that their therapist is open to data, is not prone to choose sides, and is approaching their difficulty from a problem-solving set rather than from a moralizing, directive orientation.

5 SHORT-TERM AND CRISIS INTERVENTION

In the previous chapters a number of issues considered necessary in working with couples were discussed. Indications, contraindications, reasonable expectations for intervention, and methods of assessment are all important in successful treatment. In this chapter, I will integrate those factors with strategies of intervention designed to bring about a relatively quick and satisfying return to a previously acceptable level of functioning.

This symptom-oriented approach, with the emphasis on speed and action, is found in other psychotherapies. Both individual and family therapists often emphasize symptom relief. Indeed, the most dramatic changes wrought by psychotherapists are with previously functioning people who have, as a result of stress requiring adaptation outside their repertoire of available behavior, become acutely nonfunctional. Positive change can be rapid and impressive when a functioning system, thrown out of gear by an excessive demand, is offered immediate adequate help in reducing conflict and negotiating urgent needs. The previous level of functioning may return quickly; the individual, family or couple is no longer in crisis, and the therapist can appear as a miracle worker.

Couples who present themselves to therapists are usually disillusioned and despairing. Though neither partner has given up hope for the relationship, the methods each has used to meet intense longings have been ineffectual. Each characteristically feels that the other is to blame, but there is enough uncertainty about this idea that they seek treatment together rather than divorce.

Crisis situations occur with newly married couples whose adaptive efforts lead to escalations of conflict, rather than resolution. They also occur in established relationships when a stress produces a spin-out and both partners are stuck in a position of blaming and attacking futilely. This shared behavior inevitably includes boundary-blurring and projections, as well as ineffective use of intimidation, as maladaptive mechanisms.

There is no way to achieve an immediate increase of trust; this is, at best, an evolving process resulting from satisfying experiences in negotiation. The goal of a couples therapist in a crisis situation is more modest—to increase each person's confidence in his or her own personal worth and ability to do something effective with the other. If this is accomplished, it will automatically diminish boundary confusion, as projection and blame are needed less by people who feel confident and reasonably adequate.

The therapist relies on several factors to produce a rapid recovery of couples' functioning:

1) In addition to an assessment of the individuals involved and their pattern of interaction, the therapist needs a clear statement of what each partner is seeking, both from the partner and from treatment. Though this may change as the treatment relationship develops, it is important to elicit in the beginning, since the very act of making this explicit emphasizes the focus on wishes, choices, and the resolution of ambivalence.

2) The therapist models behavior for the couple; consequently, one must have a comfortable acceptance of a wide range of human feelings in oneself as well as in others, an openness to being wrong and being corrected, a recognition

of limits that offers no hint of omniscience or omnipotence. None of these qualities precludes operating with confidence and assertiveness, however.

3) It is essential to identify the spin-out pattern of the spouses and help them become aware of it. Their awareness and their realization that either person can prevent spin-outs provide education in systems thinking.

4) It is important that the therapist make every effort to restore or increase the self-esteem of both partners.

ATTRIBUTES OF THE THERAPIST

Treating couples' difficulties requires more from a therapist than does individual psychotherapy; it also offers more latitude for genuine relationships. Dangers of intense transference and fears of sexual or other kinds of seduction are reduced by having the partners come together. Therefore, a psychoanalytic model of encouraging transference is counterproductive. A good therapist uses him/herself as a model for better interpersonal processes, as a source of rewards and punishments, and as a director and guide for the partners as they learn to interact in a more satisfying way.

In these initial interviews, designed to increase each person's confidence and to stop counterproductive attacks, the therapist can be—perhaps *must* be—assertive, forthright, and at times directive. Many good therapists are at times dramatic and develop an actor's sense of timing. These tools of the trade are respectable; to be heard and accepted is part of the task, and any method that has more potential than side effects should be considered. Being interesting is no less authentic than being dull; there is no special virtue in either, but knowing how to take or avoid center stage and choosing to do either provide therapeutic leverage.

Every effort needs to be made to develop a clear and shared context of interaction. Who invited whom to come?

Who is the initiator? What does each person want? What commitments can be expected from each person in the session? Answers to these questions are necessary to begin a clear and potentially coherent and trustworthy relationship.

I accomplish this in part by example as I state clearly why I am here, what I expect, and what I understand of the difficulty. This practical and unpretentious beginning sets the tone for a treatment experience with a knowledgeable equal, not a parental authority. People in great stress often seek me out and ask for help—and then try very hard to prove that no help is possible. The best I can offer people who are locked in combat with a loved other is the example of someone who can care and yet remain responsible for the tension within oneself. That is, caring produces a need for satisfying change in the one who is cared about. If I care for someone who is hurting, I wish to make things better, but if such change requires more than my efforts, I am dependent on the others involved in the drama for that change. I cannot make it happen; I can only encourage it. This is a very finite position indeed.

What I *can* do, after acknowledging these limits, is to resolve my own ambivalence and choose what I will and won't do, what bargains I can and cannot make. I can be directive without being frustrated if I direct as a technician: "I think this might be helpful." I do not invest my self-esteem in whether the directive is followed. If it is not followed, we have useful information. Direction, control efforts, suggestions are made as an individual equal in overt power to the partners, rather than as a superior person who is more in touch with "reality."

This is an honest position, one that offers great advantages for modeling and also keeps the therapist out of many traps. It ensures that the task is defined as "do-able," one in which a good workman can be successful and take pride. I need to be intensely aware of the elusiveness of truth, its relative nature, and the subjectivity of both perceptions and interpretations. This keeps me honest and helps me avoid getting enmeshed in marital morality plays of good guy/bad guy. It also communicates the importance of every participant's significance in a positive result.

Often patients come into couples work with grossly disparate stories and memories. Even factual material, such as frequency of events, may be remembered quite differently. "You never take me out—we haven't been dining since our honeymoon." "That is ridiculous; we were out with Doris and Don just last week." More essentially subjective material, such as feelings and emotional responses to one another, are even greater sources of controversy. "You were furious when I refused to cater to your mother." "I certainly was not angry, I was just concerned at your looking morose and resentful." A therapist who believes in some mythical objective truth may unwisely attempt to decide who distorts more and who is "healthier."

Such pronouncements as, "You wish to prove your husband a failure in order to protect your belief in your father's superiority," can be presented as the revealed Word of God, rather than the hypothesis of a behavioral scientist. Defending such an exalted position requires a verbal barrage more like that of a used car salesman than of an empathic investigator.

When observations and interpretations are made, they should appeal to data that can be shared by all participants. If possible, two or even three explanations can be offered. This allows the couple to experience the helping person as a technician rather than a god, and it encourages them to reflect and choose the most likely explanations of the behavior in question. Such exercises highlight the lack of certainty present in any person's comprehension of this complex and frequently mysterious world.

It is my experience that being assertive but not authoritarian or absolute is as useful in short-term intervention as in long-term treatment. The therapist will reward and punish in the interview session, encouraging some behaviors, discouraging others, just as spouses do during interaction. "Reward what you do want, punish what you don't want," is a statement I often make and unabashedly model. For example, pointless squabbling is painful to experience as an observer or a participant. The therapist may either suffer in silence or intervene. Sometimes the intervention must be harsh and dramatic to cut through deeply intertwined patterns of failure. On more than one occasion I have said, "If you want to bicker endlessly as you are doing here, go ahead, but don't waste your money or infest my office." In addition to its shock value, this statement forces the partners to remember that they are paying to learn new ways of functioning rather than for permission to continue the old, ineffectual ones. I have yet to see a couple leave after such a statement, probably because they too are unhappy about the continuing mess and wish for some intervention.

Usually, however, the therapist's use of reward and punishment is less vigorous and controlling. Identifying spinouts and encouraging each person to see his or her part in them allow for shared rejoicing when either partner refuses to take the next step in their grooved, repetitive struggle. (Symmetrical, sysemtic escalations)

Finally, even while I am sensitive to human ambivalence about important things, I will always emphasize basic human decency, as well as the longing for companionship and sharing that is a significant part of every person. The therapist must model for spouses the necessary skill of focusing on the side of the ambivalence one wishes to encourage. This is the source of many therapeutic techniques, from neurolinguistic programming to paradoxical interventions; all are efforts to bring out a side of the patient that is experienced by the therapist as positive.

DEMORALIZATION AND HOPE

The partners come in demoralized, having exhausted their adaptive capacities. Their hope is in the therapist, not in themselves (12). The therapist's job is to change the source of that hope from the magic of transference to the more solid material present in the couple and their relationship. This is accomplished first by discovering with the pair that major source of frustration, the spin-out pattern, identifying it clearly, and providing opportunities for each to experience his or her own capabilities in stopping a bad scene. "Either person can stop a bad scene; it does take two to make a good one." With people entering treatment, to hear and then experience that they can have some positive influence on a painful situation offers hope of a genuine sort and less reliance on magic.

A healthy respect for the pragmatic is required; what works is more important than why or who gets the credit. Troubled couples appear with a huge load of blame, defensiveness, and self-justification, and make intense appeals to and for a referee, that is, for some god-like overseer who will reward and punish according to who does the "right" thing. This is true even though repeated experiences have shown that each person's right thing has led nowhere but to further misery. The therapist who knows there are no hard and fast rules or roles that ensure success in relating begins immediately to reframe old problems into a new perspective of finding what works. This orientation is the mainstay of short-term intervention. When two unhappy people learn quickly that each can stop a bad scene if he or she chooses, this results in a rapid burst of hope and a modest sense of strength, both of which were sorely lacking. No self-exploration, no complex insights from the past can provide as much relief as this simple awareness of what one can do to avert helpless floundering.

AVERTING SPIN-OUTS

Spin-outs, described in Chapter 4, are inevitable conse-quences of marital dysfunction. It is imperative to identify them, share the information with the couple, and effectively enlist their aid in averting them.

Case Example. Mr. and Mrs. J., both 60, came into treatment be-cause he had had an affair and confessed it to Mrs. J. when his mistress became angry and threatened to call his wife. Mrs. J. was thunderstruck; though she acknowledged their marriage had been troubled for many years, with neither person very happy, she felt betrayed and violated. Mr. J. was chagrined, depressed, agitated, and extremely sensitive about having his past behavior even dis-cussed. Believing he had put his error behind him, he was becom-ing more and more distressed over his wife's preoccupation with the infidelity.

He wanted the therapist to make his wife be reasonable, count her blessings, and forget the past; she wanted the therapist to make her husband realize that she had been betrayed and that she was lovable. Their particular spin-out pattern was produced by the events surrounding the infidelity; she berated him, he became defensive, she escalated her criticisms, and so on. Im-mediate treatment consisted, in part, of helping each observe their shared pattern, noting how less defensiveness led to less hostility, and how with less berating came less defensiveness. Neither had absolute control, but each had some influence over what the other did that was so painful.

A practical, authoritative approach with a good deal of control in the initial interview can offer hope by relieving the couple of frustrating feelings of groping in the dark. After watching and listening carefully for the first few min-utes (see Chapter 4), one can usually say with some convic-tion something like, ''You both sound miserable and seem to feel helpless. Let me offer a promise. As the expert in this room, I believe either of you can learn to stop a bad scene *by yourself.* Within a very short time you can expect that these terribly draining rows will cease, because neither of you requires the cooperation of the other to bring that about. Though it takes both of you to create a good relationship, either can stop or start a miserable mess.''

The hopeful expectation is a quick stop to warfare.

Case Example. Mrs. C., a graduate student, had begun individual treatment some four weeks before a crisis prompted the visit of both marital partners. Married previously for 10 years, she had, one year earlier, divorced her first husband. Shortly thereafter she married her current husband. He had been an old boyfriend while she was still single, whose own divorce had precipitated hers; she had moved to this city in a successful effort to resume their relationship.

Following four individual sessions, in which she talked of depression, doubts, and uncertainties in her career but did not discuss her marriage, the therapist received a Sunday afternoon call from a girlfriend of Mrs. C.'s. This friend was much concerned because Mrs. C. had come to her hysterical and in a somewhat battered state after a physical fight with her husband. The therapist asked that Mrs. C. be put on the phone; she confirmed the story, stating that her husband not only had beaten her but was going to file for divorce in the morning. She agreed to come in the next afternoon and to invite her husband to accompany her.

Mrs. C., an attractive brunette with a gentle, ''good little girl'' manner, appeared with her husband, who looked truculent, sheepish, and quite wary. The therapist began with the sketchy information he had about why the three were together, saying that he understood Mrs. C. had been somewhat ''roughed up'' and that divorce was threatened. At that, Mr. C. bristled and attacked. He insisted that he hardly touched his wife, that she exaggerates and that was one of the reasons he couldn't live with her, and further, that he did not appreciate the therapist's coming to conclusions without knowing what was going on.

The therapist, ever mindful of subjective reality, quickly reiterated that he had no direct information about the events, but was, rather, sharing what he had been told so that everyone could begin at the same place. The objective, then, was to find out what was troubling the two rather than to conduct an inquisition. Mr. C. cooled down, and the interview continued. Mrs. C. described her husband's coming in on the evening of the disturbance quite drunk. He indicated that he had had only a few beers. He was, according to her, surly and insulting; she was, according to him, preoccupied and tired. She, disgusted with the drinking, poured all the liquor in the house on the kitchen floor. He rather heatedly noted that she just happened to pour it on a very important pile of legal papers dealing with the incorporation of his business.

"I didn't know that—I was just pouring it out."

"You knew exactly what you were doing—you always have resented my business. That's why I slapped you! (Not hard, Doctor) And it's also why I want out."

As the story unfolded, there had been several similar episodes in the marriage, and he had twice before filed and reversed the filing for divorce. They each had very high expectations of the other and felt betrayed and vengeful when these expectations were unmet. He needed to be in control, and his self-image encompassed being aggressive but not assaultive, though he had been beaten by his father frequently until age 17, at which time he successfully stopped the physical abuse by threatening his father in turn. She was frequently oblivious to her maneuvers, professing innocence and vulnerability and then viciously attacking his weak spots.

They agreed that each loved the other and that, if things could be better, they both wanted the marriage to continue. They also agreed that the current situation was intolerable and that neither of them knew what to do about it. At this point, the therapist asked Mr. C. how close he had come to leaving the room in the first five minutes.

"I was pretty hot, I'll tell you, Doc. I thought you were jumping on me and I didn't deserve it."

"Okay, but when I backed off and told you I wasn't there when the fight went on, that I wanted us to get current, how did you feel?"

"Well, a lot better; I believed you would listen to me."

"Fine, we nearly revved up a fight like you and Mrs. C. had, and then it collapsed. Is that right?"

"Yeah, I guess so—I'm still here."

"Then maybe we've had a small sample of something you both need to learn. That either can stop a bad scene, though it takes both of you to make a pleasant experience. I didn't want to fight and you sensed that even though you heard my words as attacking you."

Experiences accompanying words are invaluable in couples work. Concepts can be important, abstractions can be useful, but the bottom line is behavioral change, and often the couple's first experience of a different pattern is with the therapist. An effective couples therapist will use personal feelings and interaction with the partners to illustrate concepts. The purposely designed triangle provides many opportunities for intensity; the therapist must use those opportunities to provide the couple with experiences in reducing conflict and negotiating. When the C.'s experienced an escalating struggle between Mr. C. and the therapist, quite similar to their own frustrating encounters, followed by reduced tension and continued discussion, they felt more hopeful.

After that first interview, there were no more episodes of physical violence, and Mr. C. once again canceled his plan for divorce. In the following six interviews, a rudimentary systems viewpoint was established for both. She began to accept that she could be hostile, provocative, attacking and oblivous, and that these qualities were not the exclusive property of her huband. He began to see that he could be high-handed, insensitive, and demanding, and that these qualities were not exclusively possessed by his wife. As each became more aware of his or her own behavior, the sense of helplessness dissipated, hope increased, morale improved, and some satisfactions were reported. They stopped treatment after eight sessions, wanting to try to develop their relationship on their own. This couple had accepted a systemic definition of their problem: Each person was both cause and effect and each had influence on the other and on the situation; further, they had a shared concept of this particular spin-out pattern which either could derail.

Consistent with all interventions discussed in this book, the appeal is to each person's enlightened self-interest: education, not shaming or guilt induction; choice, not indoctrination. If one wants a wife who is tender and responsive rather than provocatively bitchy, one will need to be aware of her existence and express that wish. If one wants a man who is sensitive and warm, one will need to reach out without a slashing attack.

These individual response patterns are, of course, dictated by previous experiences that have developed a particular self-definition. A common factor in all of these varied experiences, however, is the assumption that people are willful and perverse, unchangeable by any but magical means, and essentially unaffected by the presenting stimuli: "You are a bad boy." "You will never amount to a thing." "You are so terribly selfish." These voices in the heads of all these people are residuals from families in which the person rather than the behavior was routinely attacked.

Individual psychology has sometimes perpetuated this orientation. "Borderline personality," "masochistic character," "hysteric neurosis"—these are labels that can apply to patients and therapists alike. Dramatic changes are possible when couples are encouraged to become conscious of needs and of altered strategies to meet those needs. In acute intervention, treatment must capitalize on the possibilities of dramatic behavioral change resulting from such cognitive learning and altered attitude sets. Almost any character structure—shy, outgoing, bold, tentative, hysteric, compulsive, etc.—can be unsuccessful or reasonably successful in living. The difference lies not in finding the proper "mature" character structure, but in taking responsibility for one's needs and finding ways to meet them.

CONFUSION AND AMBIVALENCE

In the initial session, the most frequently encountered feelings are frustration, anger, anxiety, and hopelessness. If the partners have a false sense of certainty about their respective viewpoints, tragic results may follow. The certainty is termed "false" because, with genuine resolution of mixed feelings on the part of either person, the meeting would not be taking place in a psychotherapist's office. I call this dangerous and foolish certainty "cartooning" because it leaves out all subtlety, nuance, and human complexity, revealing only the obvious and the dramatic—and usually the oppositional.

There is generally a period of confusion in the interim between false certainty and reasonable pragmatism. In fact, it is important that the therapist encourage this confusion, which results from recognition of previously denied mixed feelings, which have usually been projected onto the partner. People do not commit suicide or murder or cause bodily harm in a confused state. I make every effort to reward expressed ambivalence and to subtly challenge a "pinheaded," that is, narrow-minded, certainty. Honest reframing is a valuable tool in helping people to admit mixed feelings and to become openly confused.

Case Example. Mr. and Mrs. J., mentioned earlier in this chapter, came into treatment with a shared accumulation of dangerous false certainty. After hearing of his infidelity, she was cartooning herself as the virtuous injured person, totally free from involvement in the life that was prelude to her calamity. He cartooned himself as a pillar of virtue also; he had strayed, then repented, and was now irritated at his wife's continued harping on the past. This inverse Valentine cartoon put them on opposite sides of a bitter struggle in which neither could receive from the other. They were "running on empty," and both showed vegetative signs of depression.

A few minutes' probing revealed that she had been aware of marital pain for 25 years. Much of her satisfaction in those years had been derived from their children, who had now all left home. He had been more oblivious to problems, thinking that they had had a fine marriage until two years previously, when he felt she had ignored his efforts to communicate his emotional need. The therapist defined Mrs. J. as the "canary"—the metaphor being the bird, more sensitive than a human, that miners carry down the mineshaft to warn them of bad air. Thus, her sensitivity and hurt were framed as potentially positive and useful. The affair was defined as a great opportunity, that is, as Mr. J.'s dramatic statement that something was missing. He had conveyed to his wife that he needed her.

Such reframing was not eagerly embraced by the pair, but it threw them off balance—they were confused. He had to consider the idea that, if the affair were ignored and "forgotten," an opportunity for improving the marriage would be lost. She had to chew on the fact that until the affair all her efforts to have him acknowledge the need for improving their relationship had gone for naught. With confusion, their anxiety rose and their depression lessened. Hope was kindled as they experienced themselves on the same side, struggling with a knotty problem.

FAMILY OF ORIGIN INFORMATION

Another source of salubrious confusion is family of origin, which a therapist can productively bring out in the first few sessions—but in a special way. Couples come in with hopelessness and demoralization because of specific circumstances which they need to talk about. Keeping the focus on the here-and-now is wise, but this does not preclude asking pointed questions to elicit information about the families of each partner.

As the spouses describe their inevitably foolish, frustrating and counterproductive behavior, the therapist asks such questions as: "Hmmm. Wonder where that came from?" or, "Where did you learn to (do that) (expect that) from a man/woman?" or, "How did your father/mother handle such an event?" Such questioning, while maintaining a here-and-now focus, is another source of confusion, as each partner is forced to ask himself, "Am I responding to my spouse here-and-now and choosing my behavior, or am I programmed to see and act by experiences from the past?" Of course, the spouse will usually be a great help in developing this confusion: "You think I'm going to go behind your back like your mother does with your father." "You come at me just like your mother attacks." "You say that you are different from your father but you're not."

Sorting out these various possibilities, attacks, character assassinations, and clues to better current functioning requires a firm handle on what I have termed "systems reality." Everybody has an unconscious, including the therapist. Everybody has a family of origin, including the therapist. Everyone, including spouses and therapists, can project his or her own fantasies and memories onto a present, quite different, situation. Negotiating skill, which means boundary clarity, resolved ambivalence, and personal choice, makes for healthy families. So the therapist will model these qualities in negotiating with the partners.

Case Example. This dialogue is taken from a first session:

She: "He never says anything. He's not like people I work with now; they're articulate and assertive. I never know where he is. I enjoy my friends and my children but not him."

He: "She's never satisfied. Anything she sees on TV will make her think our marriage is lousy."

Therapist: "Is it?"

He: "No, I don't think so—we have a few problems that get recycled over and over."

She: "We never get anywhere, but that's because I feel I have to protect you—just like I had to protect my mother and father—and even my grandparents.''

Therapist: ''Oh?''

She: ''Yes. My uncle was killed in the war just as I moved in with my grandparents when I was eight. I felt I had to cheer them up—you know, I was always anxious that they might be depressed.''

Therapist: ''You must have had a hard time thinking for yourself, doing what you wanted.''

She: ''You bet. I learned my lessons well how to take care of people. But I'm different now. I like my job, my children. I just wish Tom would be more expressive.''

Therapist: ''If he would enjoy himself, you could enjoy yourself?''

She: ''That's it!''

Therapist: ''Is she right, Tom? Do you have trouble reaching for what you like, making sure you enjoy yourself?''

He: ''Every time I wanted something when I was growing up, my mother would say, 'Oh well, maybe I can give up having the kitchen redone,' or something like that. It got to where it was just too much trouble to ask for anything. My folks had money, but since they had lost everything in the Depression they were sure that times would be hard again.''

Therapist: ''So both of you have difficulty in feeling good about speaking up for yourselves?''

He and She: ''You bet.''

The focus stays on the here-and-now, but family of origin material is woven into a reframing of the problem, initially defined oppositionally, as one where both of the partners are on the same side. The stage is set for exploring difficulties with each being responsible for his or her own satisfactions.

TRUST

Love and comfort are intimately bound to trust. Couples may have lived together for years, shared sexual acts, had children together, and still profess a lack of trust in one another. Such wariness is too pervasive to be changed or healed in short-term treatment. However, as in the previous example, getting a pair to see themselves as on the same side, rather than as battling from opposite positions, is quite possible and necessary for quick improvement in the couple's trust level. Methods that promote a quick increase in the partners' relative trust by getting them on the same side may be summarized as follows:

1) Make the treatment setting a safe place to express mixed feelings and one that even rewards confusion at times.
2) Reframe behavior viewed as simple and bad to be understood as multidimensional and potentially and partly useful.
3) Discourage cartooning.
4) Develop an assumption that people are neither bad nor good.
5) Steadfastly maintain a systems view that people who live together influence, complement, and collude with each other.
6) Finally, share the belief that each partner's needs are usually the same, similar, or complementary.

Confusion and acknowledged ambivalence have a good effect on boundary problems. Accepting more of one's own feelings means that less has to be projected onto the partner. Being on the same side is really another way of saying that each person has clear boundaries and is capable of accepting the responsibility for one's life we all possess (but frequently believe we can escape by marrying!).

PRAGMATISM

Often during an initial interview I have a familiar fantasy—or perhaps it is a memory. It is summertime in Texas, before the days of air conditioning. The kitchen window is open and mother is within earshot of two four-year-olds playing in the sandbox. The pleasant chatter of the two becomes strident, tense, louder; accusations mount and one child begins to cry. There is clearly a call for help, without either child knocking on the kitchen door. The help that is hoped for is a referee who will punish the wrongdoer and reward the righteous. The problem is that each child is certain she or he is the righteous.

Sometime I share this fantasy with couples early, sometimes not. But the grown-up children who come to me are trying to solve problems in the same way the four-year-olds try—arguing, intimidating, and finally hoping for a referee. But now, for adults, there is no referee except in the risky embrace of the court system. Inviting the therapist to become that referee is not resistance or manipulation but simply a pattern learned long ago.

The pattern can be visualized as a split of wish and responsibility, with each person wanting something but placing responsibility on the other to provide it. Each finds it difficult to claim the wish because that might seem "selfish," a term each may have used as an epithet, a curse word, in reference to the other.

This fear of being selfish is also learned early. Let's set another scene with the four-year-olds. Johnny is visiting Sally and Sally is hoarding all her toys. Johnny is crying, and Mother says, "Sally, don't be selfish; share your toys with Johnny." Of course we know that mother really means, "Sally, don't be stupid. If you don't let Johnny play with your toys, he'll go home, you'll be miserable, and you'll make me miserable all afternoon." The motto, "Don't be selfish," is a shortcut in an effort to achieve a practical result by inducing guilt. Unfortunately, children may not learn that this is a parent's way of trying to be practical and selfish; instead, they grow up with guilt over their own desires and a certainty that anyone's personal advantage has to be at another's expense. This is indeed a painful belief, for if one is satisfied, then one is creating pain and deprivation in loved ones; if one behaves so as to be worthy of love, the price is personal deprivation.

The belief is common in couples who seek treatment. It is pervasive in family members who would be classified as midrange or borderline in my family classification system (see Chapter 6), and these families provide most of the people seen in couples treatment.

When the therapist challenges this assumption, the couple will quickly provide examples of the either/or satisfaction model: "I missed the party because he wouldn't go." "I missed my promotion because she wouldn't move away from her mother."

One useful and easily communicated example of a time when two people are of necessity satisfied together is sexual intercourse. If the couple has ever had a pleasant sexual experience, they readily understand that it was only as satisfying as the partner's enjoyment. If the couple has not had satisfying sex, both can usually agree that in fantasy, at any rate, sex satisfaction for one would be sex satisfaction for the other.

Another example I use is the treatment relationship. It is evident that, if I am even a modest representation of caring humanity, my satisfaction with the work is directly related to the degree that the couple sees it as rewarding. There is no way I can win except as they do, and no way they can lose except as I do. (After several years as a psychotherapist, I stumbled on a powerful motivation for me in this role: I am a most competitive person, yet I don't like to see other people lose; as a psychotherapist I have the best of both—I struggle to win and if I am successful, so are those with whom I struggle.)

Once the partners can see these instances of necessarily mutual reward, we can meet the challenge of finding out how often this same model can apply to their relationship.

It does not always apply; sometimes real conflicts of interest exist and compromise is needed. However, in most partners' interaction we will find that, as in the two examples of sex and treatment, it is erroneous to assume that satisfaction is either/or—either one or the other will lose. I arbitrarily estimate that 80 percent of the time the interaction can be mutually gratifying rather than competitive and only about 20 percent of the time does one need to seek compromise. So we now have the requirements for working with no referee, with selfishness blessed and even insisted upon, and with the pragmatic or practical as our guiding principle. I can encourage each person's efforts at resolving mixed feelings and stating what is wanted and spend more of our time together in devising successful strategies.

I have developed a method to discourage the splitting of wish and responsibility, with its resultant search for a referee and incessant efforts at intimidation and direct control. After telling a couple the stories recounted here, and listening to the problems as stated by each partner, I will say: "I will support either of you if I can understand what you want, if I think there is even an outside chance you will get it, and if *you will take the responsibility* for getting it." This does several good things. First, it underscores that selfish is beautiful. In my office it is okay to speak up for oneself. Second, it defines me as a partner, not a referee or a controller. Third, it reduces the boundary muddle of who is supposed to act on whose behalf. Responsibility and wish are firmly placed in the same person. Fourth, it cuts the ground out from under the main reason for efforts at intimidation. If one cannot place the responsibility for one's predicament on the partner, and if one cannot use a referee to do so, intimidation has little value.

Case Example. This exchange is from the couple described earlier in the section on Family of Origin Information:

She: "He is dull. I want a partner who is lively and interesting to talk with."

He: "I want her to get off my back and be satisfied with what she's got."

Therapist (to wife): "It seems to me you have several possibilities: You could give up and search for a livelier partner. You could enjoy your friends and learn to be proud that you outshine your husband. Or you could seduce, browbeat or inveigle him to be more outgoing. I would be glad to approach the problem from any of these wishes—or can you think of others?"

She (after a moment of thought): "No . . . I think that would cover it. I guess I should choose to enjoy my friends and learn to live with who he is, but that's hard."

Therapist: "Where did the 'should' come from?"

She: "Well, that's what he would say, and I guess I agree some of the time."

Therapist: "I will throw in with you in what you are trying to do when we can figure out what that is. You will be stuck with the responsibility for success, however."

He: "She is not going to give up wanting to change me."

Therapist: "You're pretty sure about that. Does a part of you want to be more outgoing, and do you use her as the voice for that part?"

Here in the first session, we are identifying mixed feelings and shared projections. We are getting gloriously confused and beginning to get some defined personal goals. I can't lean heavily on getting responsibility and wishes together quite yet, because the wishes are still unclear. Had she come in being terribly definite that she wanted him changed, the focus would be more explicitly on her responsibility for that desire, rather than on the responsibility for defining her goals.

 I find the two simple questions, "What are you trying to do?" and "How are you trying to do it?" to be invaluable touchstones to keep us all on track. When a couple comes in bickering, the question to one, "What are you trying to do?" can usually stop the dreary, painful, pointless fight.

These two questions, like the statement of my treatment bargain (my statement of being willing to support either person who wants something if that person will take responsibility for getting it), encourage a pragmatic partnership and discourage futile dreams of referees, ugly efforts at intimidation, and replays of family of origin frustrations. Nobody is all neurosis; everyone has some coping ability. It is up to the therapist to encourage each partner to experience this fact.

At this point I can hear someone saying, "If you agree to support one partner, doesn't the other partner feel left out?" Fortunately the answer is almost invariably "no" for several reasons. First, I make it clear that the offer is open to both. Second, as in the dialogue reproduced in this section, the spouses' wishes are usually complementary, not competitive. She wanted satisfaction, but when pressed did not know what that would mean. He wanted a satisfied wife, but when pressed did not know whether or not that meant he would want to change. And that leads us to the third reason: Human ambivalence being as powerful as it is, if a therapist has a system orientation and clearly doesn't believe that a marriage is composed of good guys and bad guys (for example, hysterical wives with responsible, hard-pressed husbands, or paranoid, obsessive husbands with warm, frustrated wives), his focus on their shared unhappiness resulting from relationship clumsiness gets communicated rapidly.

REPAIRING AND BUILDING SELF-ESTEEM

There are two main sources of self-esteem: 1) being heard, understood, empathized with (not necessarily agreed with), and 2) having success experiences *as defined by the person*, not by others.

Both factors have usually been in short supply in the formative years of people who enter psychotherapy. Both are important reasons for marrying—to have a sympathetic person with whom one can experience the satisfactions of successful sex and successful relating on a continuing basis. And with couples who enter treatment, these two elements are in short supply. These spouses don't seem to listen to each other and/or desperately put each other down, pointing out each other's faults. This shared behavior is accompanied by demoralization and hopelessness.

A necessary part, therefore, of marital therapy begun in crisis is the bolstering of each partner's self-esteem. A therapist with a family systems orientation is usually able to listen well and to offer dignity and respect to both persons. This is in contrast to a linear view of emotional pain and illness. Such statements as, ''She is castrating,'' or, ''He is passive-aggressive,'' encourage taking sides and result in one person's feeling misunderstood, condemned and/or labeled inferior. An interactional approach with a belief in circular causuality allows a therapist to listen and affirm the subjective reality of both spouses and then begin the vital task of translating each partner's perceptions and experiences to the other.

A systems approach to marital problems helps couples to derive success experiences that each member can achieve. With a belief in the possibility of influencing (but rarely controlling) others, the therapist models a concept of winning that is compatible with the pair's own experience of limited power.

Case Example. Mr. and Mrs. L., both age 40, came into treatment at Mrs. L.'s urging. He was a prominent professional in a medium-sized town nearby; she was an active professional woman who was also invested in maintaining a home for their two teenagers. He had moved out six months previously, stating he was dissatisfied with her lack of interest in her appearance or in any enjoyable activities. During the six months' separation, he had not progressed toward defining whether he wanted a divorce or wanted to attempt reconciliation; rather, at her urging he would say he needed time and distance. She was furious with him for keeping her dangling.

The therapist carefully noted the position and state of ambivalence of each person, several times responding to their dialogue with his understanding of the story and asking for confirmation or correction. Possible options available for each person were reviewed: He could divorce, return, continue the status quo, or define a little more clearly what would encourage him to venture home. She could divorce, continue the status quo, or rummage around in her experience, past and present, with her husband to determine whether some of the sources of his dissatisfaction perhaps reflected some dissatisfactions of her own.

With each partner, there was every attempt to be respectful of his or her particular view of the situation. There were no brickbats for his stuck ambivalence, nor were there orchids for her strong desire to maintain the marriage. Each could feel understood. In addition, there was an honest effort to define practical alternatives for each, with some alternatives phrased in a way that required little in the way of decision-making, for instance, "exploring" or "defining more clearly." In this way choice can be made for courses of action that can be successful regardless of what the other person does and *before* powerful conflicts are resolved. Couples come in wanting to jump ten-foot and twenty-foot fences while barely able to crawl; a therapist can help increase self-esteem by offering tasks that are one-foot fences. Successes with modest risks and small tasks encourage hope that the central conflicts can be resolved.

For a therapist to model good self-esteem, he or she needs to have these same pleasant experiences with the couple. The healer must arrange to be heard and affirmed also and to have the joys of success. No masochist need apply for the job of being a good couples psychotherapist! To be heard requires careful attention to moments when anxious, demoralized people are open to new possibilities and are learning to speak clearly, simply, and to the point. To succeed requires sharing decisions about treatment direction and goals with the people involved and being flexible enough to be guided by their choices. The therapist never suggests that what is stated as desired by either individual may not be so, for example, ''You say you want a sober husband, but are you sure you don't enjoy having a drunk to blame?'' A tempting ploy when a therapist feels threatened, this is likely to reduce the person's self-confidence. Although very mixed motives may be present, the therapist should operate from the assumption that everyone desires a satisfying relationship with closeness and an atmosphere of trust. This mind-set is valuable in modeling for each of the marital pair. For success in any endeavor it is necessary to imagine the desired result, hold it as an image and have confidence that there is no all-powerful obstacle in the way.

To statements such as, ''She doesn't love me; I don't care what she says,'' or, ''He doesn't want me; I don't know why he comes here,'' or, ''He's never been trustworthy, he's not trustworthy now, and he never will be,'' I immediately respond. The flow of the session stops and I say something like: ''When I want to understand people at their deepest and most elemental level, I look for ambivalence, not certainty. I have no doubt that you and your spouse at times want out of this relationship, but you both are here. I insist, if you must mindread your partner, that you read what pleases you, rather than what you dread.''

This is said with all the trappings of intensity and seriousness I can muster, and it will be repeated whenever either makes a direct, flat statement of a certainty that will guarantee defeat of a stated shared goal. Though experiences are what provide new learning, words are also important and are to be taken seriously. Self-fulfilling prophecies are the major contributors to a chronic sense of defeat, and

I will not join with someone who tells me at the outset he cannot win.

The expressions of a troubled relationship result from pessimistic mind-sets. Chronic, unresolved ambivalence, doctrinaire mistrust, projection, and depression are cognitive phenomena. Successful treatment must include a considerable amount of cognitive learning—a reshaping of current experience defined as hopeless and unrewarding into patterns that provide hope and satisfaction.

In short-term or crisis intervention with couples, there is no more important cognitive learning than an elemental systems orientation. Causes are effects and responses are stimuli each to the other. This awareness alone can do wonders with a stuck relationship and is the foundation for all other change. It is a consistent feature of capably functioning family groups.

Behavioral change occurs, however, not because of new knowledge or insight but because new behavior is tried and experienced as satisfying. As each partner enjoys his or her ability to stop a bad scene, as the helplessness of believing that the other party is totally at fault and in charge gives way to a systems approach with its hope of influencing but not controlling another's behavior, and as that behavior is truly influenced with resulting enjoyment, a more hopeful, less frustrating way of functioning follows. All of these new patterns and new rewards are related to the experience of clear boundaries that allow more clearly defined choice, as well as more influence and negotiation when another's choice is involved.

The maneuvers and strategies of the competent therapist will vary greatly with the background of the partners and their relationship. For example, couples at the upper and lower ends of the socioeconomic spectrum tend to expect directive, even authoritarian, approaches to change. Lower-class couples have frequently experienced little in the way of personal power and effectiveness in changing their situation; appeals to reflective decision-making are not comprehensible. Upper-class couples are frequently in the same situation: they come from families where one person has control of the money and all the other family members have no more sense of controlling personal destinies than do the poor. With these people, who often do not value insight, I select a more authoritative role, assigning tasks and expecting compliance. With middle-class couples, I more often negotiate conscious contracts to increase choice-making.

People also vary in their ability to convert word symbols into blueprints for action. Many couples or partners can benefit from treatment only by experiencing change during the session in the presence of the spouse and healer. This kind of learning is vital for every patient. Then there are partners who can play with abstractions, who can capture an idea and apply it outside. With the former group, I try to stay simple, emotive, strongly interactional and interventive. With the latter group, I can enjoy an opportunity to share a comprehension of reality that includes the intellect and the symbolic. Neither emphasis is wrong or right; it is the matching of method with patient styles that is important.

Even in short-term intervention, all approaches could be subsumed under the heading of increasing the couple's negotiating abilities. Nurturing hope, knowing what each person is wanting, recognizing mixed feelings, and giving up projections—all are useful. For partners to find satisfaction with each other requires continuing negotiation, much of it below awareness. As a therapist, I am always encouraged by realizing that each of these people chose each other with some feeling of magic, some satisfaction, some sense that the other was special and easier to relate to than others. Whatever they ultimately decide, each represents to the other a particular opportunity for responsible negotiation and need satisfaction. In this they are on the same side for sure.

Section Three
CHRONIC MARITAL CONFLICT

6 FRAMEWORK OF TREATMENT

HISTORICAL

The concept of romantic love in marriage is recognized to be a recent innovation and one that is peculiar to Western civilization. In other cultures, and in our own prior to the 16th century, marriage was a contract having little to do with love and much more to do with property and progeny. Nevertheless, the hunger for intense relationships is a part of the human condition. Our extended period of dependency during childhood, unique among mammalian species, unique even to all life forms, makes us long for touch and caring and being special in the eyes of another who we also think is special. The change in the last four hundred years, then, is not so much a change in the concept of romantic love between men and women, but the wholesaling of this possibility to the masses. History is filled with accounts of great love affairs, frequently between people who married, but they were of the ruling classes and never the peasantry. The industrial revolution and our own egalitarian revolution have raised the expectations of hundreds of millions of people concerning relationships, love, and marriage. Love is expected, and marriage must provide warmth and caring.

Unfortunately, markedly increased expectations for marriage have not been accompanied by the increased skills necessary to fulfill such expectations. One result has been tremendous pressure for the loosening of social, religious and legal restrictions on divorce. The current high divorce rate can be seen as a statement of the generally high hopes that people have for the institution of marriage.

With cultural history moving in the direction described, one would predict the evolution of experts in the relationship skills needed for intimacy. And here is where the connection between emotional illness and marital therapy becomes clearer. Earlier in this book I define emotional illness as a deficiency disease, a deficiency of satisfying, coherent, self-defining experiences with meaningful others. A marriage, though not the only possible place to obtain the necessary relationship "vitamins," is nevertheless the principal one for millions. Indeed, my practice includes many professional people who do not have a single friend other than their spouses.

Early in my psychiatry residency training, I became aware that treatment of serious relationship problems was handicapped by ignoring family members and working only with the person defined by the family or society as the patient. In the succeeding 25 years, I have come to the position that marital therapy can be as good as, or (usually) better than, individual treatment for the stated purposes of increasing relationship skills for intimacy—to be close, to be known. Further, these skills are the best insurance against frank emotional illness such as depression or psychosis.

We are in an era in which increasing attention is being paid to preventive measures in health care. Just as proper habits, diet, exercise and stress management have been shown to increase individual health and longevity, proper attention to the inner circle skills (referring to the circles of relationships described in Chapter 2) appears to be prophylactic for emotional illness. In addition, patients with severe emotional illness respond better to treatment when marital (or family) therapy is included. Davenport's group has shown this to be the case with bipolar illness (19,20). Goldstein et al. have demonstrated the power of utilizing spouse or family with acute schizophrenia (29), and Falloon et al. have documented similar results with chronic schizophrenic patients (23).

CHARACTERISTICS OF CONFLICTED COUPLES

Chronically unhappy couples are so because of shared, stereotyped, unrewarding behavior patterns and shared, despairing mental attitudes. People who live together have conflicts; successful couples learn how to get out of trouble and how to meet pressing individual needs in ways that do not produce even greater problems. The therapist's job is to add to each spouse's awareness, coping skills, and adaptive capacity. Such work benefits the individuals as well as helping the relationship, even in those instances in which the individuals decide to divorce. The relationship between the two is designed to serve the individuals, and therefore, a mutually agreed-upon parting serves the purposes of that relationship as well as a mutually agreed-upon committed continuation. Some marital therapists consider the dissolution of marriage to be a failure of treatment. I make a strong plea that professionals working with couples communicate their beliefs about this issue in the very first contact so that these couples can have informed consent as to treatment.

It is drearily predictable that the couple's shared behavior patterns are coercive and intimidating, each placing responsibility for difficulties on the partner and avoiding opportunities to experience individual choice. The shared attitudes, equally predictable, include doctrinaire mistrust of the inner qualities of the partner, pessimism regarding the possibilities of change, and a sense of impotence or helplessness. In addition, the specific defect of poor interpersonal boundaries, expressed by a wide variety of projective phenomena, is found routinely and dictates a major focus for successful intervention.

These patterns and attitudes represent the illness. Fortunately, every person also has areas of emotional health that can be encouraged, augmented and developed. A good therapist is alert to interpersonal skills and hopeful attitudes and reinforces them. Since each person in the troubled union has difficulty perceiving interpersonal processes and changing them for the better, education of many kinds is necessary.

Partners in unhappy marriages believe in a variety of stereotypes and feel guilty if they do not behave accordingly. Some are peculiar to a particular family, e.g., "John is a goof-off. He has talent but he never applies himself." Many are the result of a family's faithful transmission of sexual stereotypes found in the broader Western (and particularly American) culture. For example, males should be strong and silent, stupid about feelings, practical and analytical. Females should be submissive but perceptive, intuitive and illogical, indirect and untrustworthy, content to live through others and therefore happy with the goals of becoming a loving mother. More recently, a female counter-stereotype has arisen: Females should be career-oriented, express themselves through work outside the home, and fight the domination of men who try to make women homebodies.

Individuals from severely dysfunctional families and from quite healthy families are least troubled by these stereotypes. The aberrant families are too alienated from the cultural mainstream to take them seriously, and the healthy ones, not so dependent on rigid external authority, can offer children broader developmental possibilities. Stereotypes may be encountered in work with these families, but do not cause significant difficulties. It is in families that produce sane but limited children with moderate neuroses and behavior disturbances that these simplistic sexual behavioral prescriptions are more devoutly followed.

There are two reasons why these patterns are damaging

to marital relationships. First, because they are rigid and unyielding, they handicap ego development. Growing up requires all the adaptive potential we can muster, and artificial limitations are damaging. Secondly, the stereotypes force an *oppositional* limitation on male/female contacts. If males are logical, they are, by necessity, frustrated with illogical, intuitive creatures and vice versa. If females attend only to home and children and are uninterested in the broader world, they are inevitably dull to the creatures with greater vision who have little interest in the confines of the home. With the newer female stereotype, the man is an exploitative manipulator, keeping women down for his selfish benefit, and the woman becomes the natural enemy of the man.

Grim business, this! It is no wonder that millions of adults fight or withdraw their way through marriages and teach their children to grow up and do likewise.

Faced with these unconscious assumptions, the therapist begins by making them conscious and then challenging them. Helping a man admit tenderness toward his wife, a woman to express pent-up longings for competence in the larger world, allows each to see the other as similar. The more we see another as like ourselves, the greater the potential for empathy and understanding, for cooperation and negotiation.

Such an expression of the self-definition of both sexes discourages the denial of ambivalence and the projection of unadmitted feelings and attitudes onto the partner. The conventional sexual stereotypes are caricatures which make for constantly quarreling Siamese twins—two people becoming necessary to express the qualities of one real, adequately developed human being.

Some agreed-upon sex role differentiations are helpful, however. Complementary rules and tasks are necessary to avoid continuing strife. Conventional or unconventional, they are needed. Somebody needs to be primarily responsible for the various areas of shared living—cleaning, yard work, child care, food preparation, making the money, tidying. Cleaning may be broken up into bathroom, living room, kitchen. Yard work may be divided into lawn mowing, shrubbery watering and trimming, but clear bargains concerning areas of responsibility and specific territory are required for making simple things simple. These roles and tasks vary with different families, and every newly committed couple has extensive negotiating to do regarding them. Serious problems arise when the negotiating is based on presumed absolutes, complicated even further by tying the absolutes to sexual identity.

In a society that changes slowly, sex stereotyping is beneficial as it simplifies the definition of rules and territories. In our rapidly changing social structure, its far-reaching changes illustrated by statistics regarding working women, female heads of families, divorce and remarriage rates, flexibility is essential for adaptability. Neither old or new stereotyping is helpful, although complementary tasks remain necessary and partners' ability to negotiate their particular needs is at a premium.

With society in flux, there is no generally accepted norm for individual behavior. The conservatism of the family, a product of the strong pull for identification with parents, its ritual and sense of "rightness" dependent on childhood memories, is therefore a two-edged blade. We need security in a tempest, yet we need to grow and change in order to adapt. To see the importance of both and to encourage patients to accept the inevitable tension within themselves from these conflicting needs are challenging tasks for the therapist.

It is of limited value to compile separate lists of personality types seen in wives and husbands. Any personality type can be successful and any can fail. Shy people, aggressive people, "cold fish" and sensuous women can be found enjoying their grandchildren, talking to psychiatrists or visiting divorce courts. Growth-promoting therapy with couples (or individuals) does not consist of developing common "mature" personalities, but rather, of assisting individuals to define and achieve their personal goals within the capabilities of their particular styles. Any experienced couples therapist has noted the frequent, sometimes confusing, switches in expressed "personality" couples can make. He will be compulsive and cold, she, flighty and emotive; two weeks later they return and she is rigid and tensely withdrawn, overcontrolled and controlling, while he is agitated, overwrought and dramatically emotional. Diagnosis of personality is made on shifting sand, and precision in such diagnosis is an illusion not compatible with an interactive systemic orientation. The *patterns* are stereotyped, but partners will frequently switch roles within that pattern of interaction.

Treatment, then, naturally follows from the diagnostic appraisal. Boundary confusion is clarified, power differentials are reduced, and intimacy becomes possible. In the following pages I will list specific interactional variables, ranging from the most dysfunctional to the least. Let me emphasize once again that emotional illness is here defined as a deficiency of coherent, satisfying, self-defining experiences; treating chronic marital discord is a way of healing that deficiency by enabling the partners to have new and satisfying experiences with each other and with the therapist.

DISTINGUISHING ACUTE FROM CHRONIC CONFLICT

There are three major factors in separating acute from chronic marital conflict. These are: 1) the circumstances of treatment, 2) the definition stated by the couple, and 3) the quality of relationship skills possessed by the pair. Note that the skills or, inversely, the "pathology" of the couple is only one factor and often not the most significant one in this distinction.

Many treatment settings and some concepts of therapy define all problems as acute. Overburdened public clinics are frequently able to offer only crisis intervention and therefore ignore the chronic relationship ineptness that leads to recurrent crises. Making a virtue out of necessity, concepts of treatment arising from such environments place a high value on short-term treatment and state or imply that intensive long-term treatment is bad, indulging either the therapist or the patients.

Conversely, some private settings encourage the definition of any marital problem as chronic. Since relationship skills are like tennis or golf skills, in that everyone has room for improvement, psychotherapists may focus on deficits rather than strengths and urge lengthy treatment. (It is important that the training of marital and family therapists include both the context of short-term, "in and out" treatment and the opportunity to resolve chronic conflict.)

The second factor, the choice of the couple, allows a negotiated definition of acute or chronic in those treatment settings which recognize both. I often see couples with reasonably adequate skills in relating to each other who want more and are willing to pay for the help, even though they are not despairing or on the brink of divorce. At least as frequently, I see couples who take a "flight into health" after a crisis is over. These choices are related to family of origin styles as well as individual preference (more about family styles comes later).

Finally, the competence or ineptness of the couple is influential in determining chronicity. Many partners come from families so restricted in living skills, with individual members so emotionally deprived, that chronic friction is inevitable, no matter how a clinic or the individuals might choose to define the situation.

DEVELOPMENTAL FRAMEWORK

The related concepts of boundaries, projections and symbiosis together form an umbrella which integrates the theoretical approaches mentioned above and helps the therapist comprehend various marital problems within a developmental framework. With the increasing influence of ego psychology, boundary issues—the differentiation of the ego or self which is a vital part of psychic development—occupy a prominent place. Projective phenomena, originally an analytic concept, have been incorporated by treatment theories of all sorts. Boundary issues are a vital aspect of systems concepts, and projection is recognized as a powerful means of subverting boundaries in family systems.

Though the concepts are not usually explicit in behavior therapy, all of the interventive procedures developed by the behavioral approach require a clear-cut difference between the change inducer and the responder—therapist and patient, parent and child, or spouse and partner. Confusion as to who is wanting to do what to whom will destroy the usefulness of these specific treatment techniques.

Chronic marital discord is intimately associated with poor delineation of self boundaries, with a variety of projections onto the spouse and with the frequent perseveration of a symbiotic relationship, all of these being similar to processes hypothesized as normal in early childhood development.

The level of differentiation and boundary clarity varies widely among couples; also, two marital partners, with their unique family histories, will have had different experiences in regulating self boundaries. A therapist who encounters partners who both come from severely disturbed families will find it necessary to work on basic, simple boundary issues, for example: Who is feeling what? Who wants what? Which person is in pain? Who is motivated to change? Who is saying what at this particular time? Coherence is the primary need, and boundary clarification can provide it.

Further up the scale of individual development and, hence, of the family and couple system, the focus is on control issues. With these couples the therapist encourages each person to become aware of intimidation and its alternatives. The desire for intimacy and the skills required to obtain it occupy much of the treatment time. Spouses often begin with severe boundary confusion and, as they evolve, later attempt to deal with the loss of intimacy resulting from pervasive efforts at control without negotiation. In these varied degrees of relationship disturbance, however, one can see a common thread, a consistent symbiotic quality in chronic marital discord. Each partner uses the other both as an excuse for his or her own personal defects and as the source of needed love and warmth. Frequent projections destroy boundary integrity and result in an unfulfilling, drearily repetitive relationship that can be neither improved nor given up.

Individual personality development can be classified according to the degree to which the first relationship that humans know—mother/infant—is maintained or replaced. This initial relationship is one where impotence and omnipotence exist simultaneously in both people. The baby is totally helpless, yet that very helplessness tyrannizes the mother and binds her to the task of caring for baby. Mother is powerful and yet must forego her own pleasures for the child's needs. Normal development consists of the gradual elimination of this kind of interaction. Its continuation in adulthood indicates the presence of emotional illness. Psychosis, viewed interpersonally, is a pervasive return to or maintenance of the omnipotent/impotent relationship pattern; neurosis and behavior disorders reflect the same pattern in a portion of an individual's life. This perception of emotional illness dramatizes its essentially interpersonal expression. The marital partner is frequently chosen to play out the drama.

From the impotent/omnipotent pattern, interpersonal relationships develop toward competent patterns, in which there is rarely helplessness and never omnipotence (or absolute power) in achieving desires and goals. Boundaries are respected and individuals experience personal dignity. Spouses engaged in a painful, unrewarding, and competitive relationship pattern usually try to change things by relying once again on the impotent/omnipotent approach that got them into trouble; they need help to develop shared goals and cooperative efforts.

It is probably clear by this point that I consider an essential part of the treatment of chronic marital discord to be *necessarily* the assistance of individual self-development. Increasing autonomy and the evolution of choice are the twin goals of individual growth. Negotiation between partners requires acceptance of personal responsibility as well as respect for each other's perceptions and needs. Furthermore, there is no inevitable conflict between individual growth and couples treatment: One complements the other, or both go awry. To feel that personal suffering and deprivation are the price for being loving and generous, that is, the belief that "my happiness comes out of your hide" and vice versa, is an erroneous but powerful self-fulfilling prophecy.

FAMILY PATTERNS OF DISCORDANT COUPLES

Chapter 2 refers to a family assessment schema used for understanding and communicating family characteristics. The following is a more complete presentation of the conceptual framework which has guided my work with couples and families. Those who wish to pursue the subject and perhaps use the rating scale in their own practice are referred elsewhere for more details (5,6,13). The schema is based on family systems theory and emphasizes family competence in problem-solving and conflict resolution. It also determines the current family style. Together these aspects form a coherent description of the family that is useful for research and clinical purposes.

The family is asked to perform a 10-minute task; non-labeled families play together or plan something together, while clinical families discuss what they would like to see changed in their family. This family assessment approach utilizes primarily direct observation of interaction; it is augmented in our own clinical practice and teaching by careful family interviewing, as well as by self-report questionnaires.

There are important characteristics of this model resulting from its evolution from general systems theory. These include:

1) Its use of *continua*, rather than discrete "types." Most of the potential destructiveness of labeling comes from attempting to put a varying, interacting universe into small boxes and then developing a Procrustean bed to force fits.
2) *Functioning*, not form, is the key word in competence. Families may have a similar level of current performance with a variety of styles.
3) Systems properties can best be determined by observers of the system in action rather than by members of that system. Figure 1 is a visual description of the family schema.

The competence continuum is horizontal, with optimal families in the first fifth of the area and adequate families in the second fifth. As a therapist, one seldom sees these families or couples. Midrange families, with their emphasis on control and with offspring who are sane but limited,

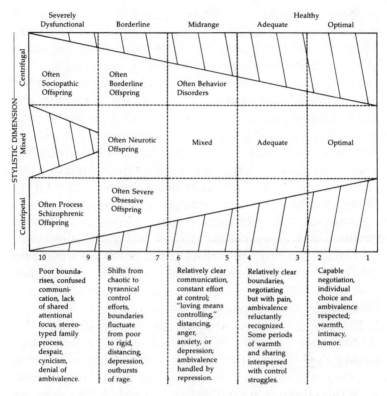

Figure 1

often having neurotic or moderate behavior problems, occupy the center. We have found borderline families to be significantly different from either midrange or severely dysfunctional families; therefore, they are given a place of their own. They have communicational deficits and problems with coherence similar to severely dysfunctional families, but these communications problems are interrupted and modified by intense control efforts.

Severely dysfunctional family members have serious difficulty in encountering one another; their communicational problems are great, their conversation generally incoherent not only to outsiders but to family members themselves. They operate as if there is terrible danger in making sense to one another about important feelings and issues.

This model also measures the family style on what we have termed, after Stierlin (45), *the Centripetal/Centrifugal (CP/CF) dimension*. This dimension is related to Olson's term *cohesiveness* (41) and to Minuchin's concepts of *enmeshment* and *disengagement* (38). However, it is important to develop vocabulary specific to the different relevant systems levels. The terms centripetal and centrifugal are especially fitting as language to describe characteristics of a group.

CP families look primarily for satisfaction within the home; CF families expect gratification to be found outside the home. CP family rules favor the expression of positive feelings and discourage the direct expression of hostility. CF family rules handle hostility well but have trouble accommodating expressions of tenderness, fear, need, and dependency.

The diagram is in the shape of an arrow to illustrate the concept that "systems sickness is a system rigidity," as stated by von Bertalanffy (16); that is, the healthier and more adaptive the family, the less significant is the current style, since the family is able to change if needed. The extreme forms of CP/CF family styles are seen only in rigid and poorly functioning families whose stereotyped patterning demands a simple style. There is no mixed CP/CF category in the severely dysfunctional and borderline families for the same reason.

The most significant variables include:

1) negotiation and task performance;
2) conflict resolution;
3) feeling tone and expressiveness;
4) communication patterns that indicate interpersonal boundary development and individuation; and

5) the style of suppressing or allowing positive or negative feelings.

Midrange centrifugal families are rarely seen in any treatment setting, as their family members consider the difficulties that they have to be part of living and handle them by acting, not talking. Their pain and dysfunction are not sufficient, nor do these individuals possess the discipline and the trust in relationships and in words required for individual, couple, or family treatment. If my practice and those of my close colleagues are representative, midrange centripetal families provide nearly half of the patients seen in marital therapy. These families are control oriented; they believe that loving means controlling. Selfish is equated with evil, and since everyone (other than a few suicidal chronic schizophrenics) can be shown to be selfish, this is seen as evidence of mankind's basic malevolence. These family members believe that one person's advantage comes out of another's forebearance and suffering. It is in this group that current cultural sexual stereotypes are incorporated and most visible. They also tend to consider all family relationships as necessarily unequal in overt power, since a basically evil nature would require external control (for oneself as well as for others) as a prerequisite for peace.

Nevertheless, these families have inklings of something better, something warm and loving. Intimacy creeps in, like grass through cracks in city sidewalks. Friendships with egalitarian qualities are frequent outside the family, and these can be utilized as models for non-intimidating family and couple bonds.

Midrange mixed families are becoming more frequent therapy clients. These are typically "shell middle-class," where the families of both parents were clearly CP and possessed traditional middle-class values regarding work and sexual roles. The families of origin were usually in small towns; however, the children of these traditional families have grown up, moved to a city and, as they have had children, developed a two-income family. Both parents are preoccupied with work, young children are cared for in groups outside the home, and older children are alone after school before parents come home from work. These parents try to use the controlling parental methods of their own families of origin, which worked because of the great amount of personal contact between parents and children. Without the thousands of hours of contact the children are likely to respond to intimidation efforts with sullen misbehavior. Parents then feel cheated out of many satisfactions and view the children as troublesome and ungrateful.

When I began with this model, borderline families were not defined as a separate group, and midrange and severely dysfunctional families were the only competence-related clinical entities. It has since become clearer that a large group of families are definitely less confident and more difficult to treat than midrange families, yet do not show the severe problems in coherent communication seen in the severely dysfunctional families. This group, found along the border between the two original groups, is termed borderline, and these families are characterized by two extreme and paradoxical qualities—chaos and rigidity. That is, these families show short-lived qualities of zaniness and dizzying incoherence worthy of severely dysfunctional families, supplanted by truly awesome efforts at control and intimidation.

In general, the CF borderline families have a history of being unsuccessful in their effort at control through intimidation, while the CP families are historically quite effective not only in stopping a crazy interlude by controlling and being controlled but also in controlling the future behavior of a spouse or a child in this fashion. One interesting clinical footnote: It is these borderline CP families that produce almost all anorexic patients and many bulimics.

This borderline group sacrifices satisfaction for efforts at control; as a result, they are clearly more despairing and more depressed than midrange family members.

Severely dysfunctional families are the most despairing of all the groups, evidencing extreme pessimism to the point of cynicism. Their communication is peculiarly ineffective; they talk as if a genuine open and intimate encounter would destroy one of the participants. In fact, that is what these family members believe; ordinary human attributes are construed as threatening to life itself. The belief of these families is, "Loving means thinking and feeling just alike," so that all members have the nightmarish choice of being honest and a pariah or being safe and constantly dissembling, believing that no one, not even close family members, knows who the other is, what he or she believes and feels.

A variety of complex verbal mechanisms maintains this uneasy balance—sarcasm, irony, disqualifications, shifts (that is, stating one side of an ambivalent set of feelings, then, without any transition or effort at coherence, stating the other).

Severely dysfunctional CF family members express hostility quite well; they cannot own up to fear, need, and love of the other family members. They will not come together easily as a family; often their therapist starts with one individual, frequently compelled by one being in school, jail, or a mental hospital. With hard work, others of the family can be coaxed or seduced into treatment.

In contrast severely dysfunctional CP families are happy to come together for treatment and will make great sacrifices to do so. Self-direction and leaving home are seen as the ultimate threat and sin; consequently, a therapist can find that such a family cooperates in treatment and yet experiences little change or movement. Coherence is longed for and yet feared; with coherence comes understanding, knowing each other, and the possibility of negotiating and resolving conflicts; it also means exposure, and the threat of expulsion.

FAMILY LIFE CYCLES

Though family and marital patterns have a strong gyroscopic tendency, that is, they tend to endure, there are special developmental challenges that couples must meet as the family evolves in order to remain stable and gratified. These challenges are usually met well by competent families and poorly by the more inept, but there are differences in response to particular challenges that are related to family makeup. Just as a surgeon would be more threatened than a psychiatrist by the loss of an arm, for example, so are achievement-oriented families more stressed by the breadwinner's job loss or the demands of an aged parent's care than families without intense desires for upward mobility.

Boss has provided a chart of normative transitions for couples, which she terms "life span boundary changes" (17). She is viewing family life cycle changes from the vantage point of boundaries between family members and those outside. The changes include formation of the dyad, birth of the first child, children first going to school, job-related parent/spouse absence or presence, adolescent children leaving home, taking in children not your own or blending children from different dyads, loss of a spouse, loss of parents, remarriage or remaining single.

Formation of the dyad requires leaving home, a clear renunciation of being a child in the family of origin and becoming an adult in a new household. Though this challenge is a continuing one, it is highlighted in the formative stage of a new family; sometimes a spouse is co-opted into a family of origin much as another sibling, rather than the marriage being the developmentally sound result of both partners' becoming adult. Family loyalties become confusing when loyalty to one's parents seems to require remaining a child. In every aspect of family life, triangulation is a challenge to be handled; if the husband-wife bond is weakened by ties to the family of origin, the new structure is, of course, threatened.

The birth of the first child offers a second dramatic challenge to the couple, again with the threat of triangulation. Mother and infant can become a tight combination coexistent with an alienated husband/father. This is a particularly stressful time for new fathers, with frequent desertions, alcoholic binges, and other evidences of alienation and stress.

When children first go to school, parents experience the inevitable awareness of loss resulting from growth and development. As much as small children get in the way and require large amounts of attention and involvement, evidence of autonomy represented by attending school is painful and can alter family dynamics and challenge stability.

Job-related absences are increasingly common for both sexes. With currently 63% of women over 16 in the work force, with the prediction for this to be 75% by 1995, spouses have to deal more and more with absences of a partner for varied lengths of time. This stresses the couple dyad and requires a wider range of adaptiveness than was demanded in simpler times with fewer job opportunities or job pressures on both spouses.

When adolescent children leave home, the cycle is beginning to turn around and parents are in the opposite role of letting go, rather than struggling to get loose as they did during their own adolescence. Many families have handled developmental stresses well up to this point, and then the system goes awry as, for example, mother finds she has depended on a child or children for company and self-definition and the marital dyad has long been sterile. Or father finds he has depended on children for stimulation and without them the marriage is depressing.

With a higher divorce and remarriage rate, taking in children not your own is ever more frequent. Particular challenges to adapting are produced by this change from the
nuclear family. For example, with nonbiological offspring,
parental discipline is more difficult to carry out, and many
remarried couples' problems result from strong but unresolved ambivalence over wanting to discipline or wanting
the spouse to help discipline and yet feeling resentful of being called upon to be the "heavy," the enforcer. There are
many more subtleties of relationships with stepchildren,
half-siblings, or foster children; sometimes the children themselves cope more easily with these than do their parents.
Boundary problems are exquisitely sensitive when a child
lives part of the time in one home and part of the time in
another with very different family rules and limits. Mental
health professionals have a great deal to learn in this area
in order to do well by their patients and clients.

As the family ages, loss of a spouse is to be expected, and
that spouse statistically will be the male. Women on average
can expect eight years of widowhood. The adaptive demands
for establishing a meaningful network outside the dyad are
only accentuated by the loss of a spouse. Outside networks
are necessary prior to such a loss in order for the couple to
maintain good morale, optimism, and a sense of well-being.
"Gruesome twosomes" can work well for periods of time
but are most vulnerable to becoming disturbed when they
have no one but each other available to express the inevitable
negative feelings. Just as working for a good marriage will
also help the individuals if divorce is to be the decision,
couples who successfully avoid the empty nest syndrome
and enlarge their group of valuable and loved friends will
inadvertently help the survivor's adaptation.

Family changes occur with the expected loss of parents
and the diminished competence of those parents. Children

become parents to their own parents, and couple relationships can be threatened when aged, infirm and frequently frustrating and tedious parents must be dealt with. Many upwardly mobile couples, after having dealt successfully with the basic inefficiency of their children (play and silliness and touching and time to grow up are necessarily inefficient), founder with the somewhat similar demands for inefficiency required in relating to the aged. Children and old people have much to teach us, but we often are too busy to notice; marital stress can increase as the pressure for accomplishment interferes with the pressure of needful elders. The death of parents can also trigger regression and system conflict, particularly if members of couples have little experience or modeling of effective mourning.

Finally, there is a special couples problem after the death of a spouse in deciding whether to remarry or to remain single. The survivor may be concerned about which choice would be truly faithful to the dead spouse. Further, there is considerable risk in establishing a new bond with a person who has had a long and very different life. The new marriages of older couples present tremendous challenges in negotiating new family rules and new ways of doing simple everyday things.

SUMMARY

This chapter takes up a variety of elements that are important in the evolution, definition and treatment of chronic marital conflict. The history of our society influences our expectations of marriage and of our spouses. Tragically, our social skills vary inversely with our needs for another, and deficits in obtaining intimacy produce chronic marital conflict and can be a powerful factor in severe emotional illness.

The degree of competence in the present family and in families of origin plays a large part in the pain or satisfaction found in marriage. Although negotiating skills will help couples handle all the expected crises occurring during a family life cycle, couples and families differ in vulnerability at the various stages.

7 COMMON PROBLEMS AND SOLUTIONS

TOOLS OF THE TRADE

A capable couples therapist uses a variety of concepts, approaches, and techniques that can all exist compatibly under the umbrella of a multilevel systems approach. These same concepts and methods have been the object of Balkanization and counterproductive conflicts among therapists. Family therapists attack the psychoanalytic practitioner, behavior therapists attack both, and existential therapists may believe they have no definite concepts or technique.

By now I hope it is evident that I believe we live in a multilevel world and must take into account culture, institutions, family dynamics, dyadic patterns, individual intrapsychic reality, and biological possibilities and limits. A good couples therapist, thinking systems, will be shuttling between various levels as she or he works, including the person of the therapist in and out of the system attended, using techniques that might be labeled psychoanalytic, behavioral, systemic, educational or elementary. The systems therapist is an "alley fighter," using the approach that seems most useful and sensible. There is a structure to this eclecticism, however; individual differentiation and choice-making, equal-powered transactions which allow for intimacy, sharing that increases warmth and a sense of belonging—these are goals of treatment in addition to whatever symptoms and requests a couple presents.

Psychoanalytic, behavioral, communicational, and specific family techniques are useful but limited if attempted as a single approach. In the following pages, I describe interventions that include many approaches and offer a rationale for using one or another at particular times. A given therapeutic maneuver may encompass several, and an adherent of each theoretical approach could interpret an intervention in the light of that theory. For example, consider this interaction:

He: "You know, just like we talked about last week, I really have just assumed Jane will turn me down if I ask her directly for anything at all. This is what happened between me and my mother—she never had time for me. I asked Jane directly for some time and attention and it worked! She really was nice to me."
Therapist: "Hurray! I'm delighted that you found a way to experience your wife as warm and rewarding!"

This exchange combines interpretation of now vs. then, new awareness of an interpersonal aspect of the relationship, and direct reward, both at home and in the therapist's office. Therapists, like early barnstorming pilots, have dealt with such complexity "by the seat of their pants." A manual of couples therapy is an attempt to make the process more conscious and more explicit.

Notice that the therapist was rejoicing with the patient for a success as *defined by the patient*. This extremely important element of direct, positive response by a therapist will add warmth, enthusiasm, and a welcome sense of shared success. It is sharply contrasted with warmly responding to behavior which is *appealing to the therapist* but not an explicit choice of the patient, thus encouraging a parental role for the therapist and a child's role for the clients. This one-up/one-down situation must be avoided in growth-promoting treatment. As the clinician moves from intervening in acute and crisis situations to promoting relationship skills, self-esteem, and appreciation of the human world, he may wisely choose to confirm himself as a technician with specific knowledge but no more overt power than the client. Problems may then be defined and solutions explored without recourse to fixed, authoritarian solutions.

GOALS OF THE THERAPIST

When a couple begins treatment, the therapist will press for explicit goals from each partner. This is a necessary part of successful treatment that allows for practice in self-definition and in negotiation. The therapist also has goals, which can be broadly defined as evolving attitudes and interpersonal processes that facilitate individual choice and goal attainment in personal relationships. These legitimate and necessary treatment goals specifically include:

1) instilling hope,
2) increasing relative trust between people chosen as possible intimates,
3) increasing self-esteem of the partners,
4) increasing their interpersonal skills, and thereby
5) increasing their satisfaction in living.

CONTEXT AND CONTRACTS

Unless all three people in the treatment relationship have a reasonably clear shared idea of what each person wants to do and agrees to do or not do, treatment may perpetuate the difficulties. Here the therapist can lead the way and be a good role model for coherence.

After initial complaints have been aired, the therapist may begin: "You both seem to be in emotional pain; I would like to help. Are you both wanting to work on the relationship? That is, are you both hopeful that the relationship can be maintained?" If each person can openly state that she or he *wants to see if they can live together happily,* there is a solid basis for treatment, with each partner expressing a personal goal and one goal shared by both. (Please remember this is a far cry from asking a member of a painful marriage to say that she or he wants to stay married, an impossible decision for most of these demoralized, shell-shocked victims.) A variety of deceptive maneuvers and confusing communication may ensue: "I don't want any more of what I've had." "She blames me for everything and I'm fed up." "He wants out, but doesn't have the guts to admit it." "She doesn't love me; she doesn't know how to love." It is important to sort patiently through these verbal weeds and obtain some coherent statement about individual goals and an underlying shared purpose.

The therapist continues: "Okay, so you both agree that divorce is a possibility, but you both want to see if you can keep your relationship and find it enjoyable. Is that correct?" The partners then find that in the midst of the hostility, demoralization and despair, they do have a shared curiosity and some hope. Without making this explicit, a therapist is not likely to do much of value. For any couple who chooses a therapist rather than a lawyer, the hope usually exists, but unless the situation demands its expression, each person will try to hide and deny this hope the way wary boxers guard their vulnerable parts.

Eliciting the shared commitment to explore possibilities in good faith (usually in one to three sessions) begins the modeling of negotiation skills. However, I remember one couple with such ongoing contextual confusion that two years were required to reach this point. After two conjoint sessions failed to clarify this issue, I referred the husband to a colleague and I worked with the wife individually until they could decide to explore relationship possibilities together. Though their arrival together for the first session reflected some desire on each person's part to continue the marriage, the wife had filed for divorce and that divorce action was in continuance for the two years of her individual treatment.

Many people have learned from their primary families that the blurring of context is protective rather than alienating. The therapist must insist on clarity of expressed purpose. After their initial success with coherent goal definition, couples often retreat into mutually confusing interaction as they discuss particular problems and resentments. One of these maneuvers includes invasiveness, the disqualification of another's experience by speaking for that other.

Case Example. These partners think they know one another's minds:

She: "He never wants to talk about our problems, and I get so frustrated. Whenever I want to talk seriously, he thinks I'm a bitch."

"Honey, I don't think you are a bitch; you just want to talk at bad times."

Is the therapist dealing with an oblivious husband, a paranoid wife, both, or neither? When this wife was asked, "Did anybody in your family often speak for the other person?" she immediately and angrily responded that her mother never let anybody speak for himself. In a short time, she was startled to see herself behaving like this mother she so resented.

Asked if he remembered dodging encounters when growing up, the husband responded, "Well, yeah. My mother was never satisfied, always suffering, the martyr type. She blamed my dad for never having any money, and he would just take his hat and leave. I learned to do the same thing with my mother; she was hard to stay around."

In the foregoing example, some of the multiple approaches to treatment are illustrated:

1) *Developing awareness of patterned behavior.* The wife was aware neither of her invasiveness nor of this pattern's being like her mother's, but inviting her to remember if she

had experienced a similar pattern produced insight and awareness. She soon began to catch herself when speaking for another. Invariably, such invasive statements to a spouse conjure up negative—not positive—feelings, thoughts or motives. I make a rule that if one speaks for another, the line must be at least positive! Here, for example, I asked the wife to invade by saying, "He really thinks I'm courageous to want to talk about our problems." This, of course, took all the pessimistic "fun" out of the invasion. It also broke the pattern learned from her mother.

2) *Clarifying the confusion of then and now.* She had played out with her husband a drama that had been experienced with her father and mother. He had automatically assumed that his wife would be as dreary in encounter as his mother had been. Comparing "now" with "then" is most important in sharpening the awareness of now and the meaning of then.

3) *New learning.* The awareness of a distancing pattern (i.e., she invades, he withdraws) allows more effective behavior to be explored; she can ask, he can risk involvement, and the results can be brought to therapy as successes or new puzzles to be explored.

A frequent gambit in confusing context is the use of questions which are really statements not claimed by the speaker.

She: "Why do you always think the worst of me?"
He: "Why can't you be like other wives and be happy to stay home?"
She: "Why don't you ever want to go out?"

Nothing good will ever result from discussion proceeding from these confusing and truly irresponsible beginnings, from which the attacker can backtrack and deny: "I never said you always think badly of me." "I never said you aren't like other wives." "I never said we never go out."

The therapist can model contextual clarity by asking repeatedly: "What are you trying to do?" "How are you attempting to accomplish it?" Such intervention may be frequent. With the first illustration: "Wait a minute, what are you trying to do? Do you want to complain that he thinks badly of you? Or do you want him to think well of you?" With the second: "Do you wish to complain about your wife's desire to go out, or the frequency that she does go out, or are you wanting her to be at home? Or are you wanting her to want to be at home?" In clarifying the desires of each person, the therapist often must be very active. If the therapist is confused, it is highly possible that the discourse will go nowhere. Coherence can be developed only if the therapist is willing to struggle for it and remains alert to confusing statements that convey emotional power but little else. One must develop an ambiance that is receptive and friendly to openness and clarity and makes obfuscation painful and difficult.

Other communicational gambits used to create a murky mess that precludes change include: invasiveness, shifts, silence, sarcasm, irony and hostile humor, and irrelevant counterattacks.

The shift is the expression of one's viewpoint followed by stating the opposite position without any of the bridging words that acknowledge ambivalence. It forces the listener to take all the responsibility for deciphering the speaker's position and is particularly disorienting. This maneuver is rare in families more competent than borderline. For example, a wife states, "I certainly do want a child. My work is engrossing and my career is demanding. I'll get no help from John in caring for a baby. There's no way it would work out well."

Becoming an expert at clarifying communication allows a therapist to sharpen issues and to help couples who feel stuck and defeated to resolve conflict and develop hope. For example:

She: "Did you get the car fixed?"
He: "You're always on my back!"
Therapist: "John, did you feel that was an honest question?"

A systems viewpoint assures the therapist that there are no cops or robbers, just victims, in these frustrating maneuvers. She may have known about his failure to fix the car and he answered her implicit attack, or it may have been an honest question which he evaded. Many such encounters and clarifications may be needed before both partners realize that the therapist is not judgmental but an investigator of problems, that there is no objective reality but only a shared one. If any of the three feels maneuvered, manipulated or controlled, that feeling must be explored. Is it from now or then? Is there current reason, or is it a hangover from the past?

Silence, sarcasm and irony are weapons to produce ambiguity. Disdainful silence is used by a partner who seeks greater social power to hide fear and a sense of helplessness; submissive silence can hide control efforts. Examples:

She: "He never wants me sexually or any other way; he doesn't love me or need me. I'm at the end of my rope."
He: silence.
Therapist: "John, how did you feel when Susan said that?"
He: "I'm glad she is able to express that—to get it off her chest."
A therapist must be persistent with such maneuvers: "Okay, John, but is she correct? She is saying you don't need her or want her, and she is speaking for you. Is this true? Can you speak for yourself?"
The therapist takes the implicit question of the partner and makes it explicit. He can do that because he has the underlying belief that honesty and clarity are valuable, and that human vulnerability and need for others are universal. Troubled couples often do not believe this. Usually the result of such a confrontation is something like this:

John: "Of course I need her and I love her too, but she pushes and pesters me and I get mad and don't say anything."

Sarcasm, irony and hostile humor stir the confused context found in chronic marital discord. These are the tools of people who feel impotent to express feelings that would be challenged and perhaps produce a hostile exchange. The statements are multileveled, complex, ambiguous, and distancing. The therapist must call attention to such comments, since these maneuvers, though powerful, are usually unconscious.

She: "Of course, my husband never does anything wrong" (voice dripping with sarcasm).
He: "Naturally, since my wife comes from a banking family, my efforts to handle money are bungling" (said with a dry ironic twist).
He: "My wife's always trying to improve herself. She's had six majors in two years of college. Not many people can top that!"

Humor can be a leavening factor in the tragedy of living, with its inevitable pratfalls and final defeat in death. But a valuable family rule of thumb is to joke about strengths, not weaknesses, about areas of clarity and comfort rather than those of unresolved conflict and pain. This rule can be developed and partners can learn that, when dealing with passionate issues and powerful conflicts, being simple and honest is productive.

New learning of this sort is effective; as one partner refuses a provocative invitation to some frustrating no-win treadmill, the other will usually respond with appreciation. This is true especially if the response is soft, acknowledges shared need, and above all clarifies the position of the speaker.

The therapist is a continual model for change. She or he cannot afford to use silence and verbal confusion and must be aware of the destructive potential of these mechanisms whether utilized by a therapist or by marital partners. Being simple and clear is not easy and may even be avoided in the mistaken belief it is childlike or naive or unprofessional.

The desired clarity leaves plenty of room for ambivalence. Marital partners from severely dysfunctional families usually believe that people, at their core, have one feeling. "He hits me sometimes, but I know he really loves me, deep down." "She says she loves me, but I know that is just a front." This dangerous and erroneous belief in one "real" feeling is the source of much complex multilevel incoherence, since, in their depths, people are ambivalent and can express such mixed feelings clearly (and so can a therapist).

The belief that spouses, therapists, or patients can be all things—lover, mother, son, friend, victim and persecutor—is the most powerful source of purposeful confusion of context. In order to have marital partners struggle to clarify their roles, intentions and expectations, that clarification must produce new satisfaction. Giving up an expectation that a spouse will be a parent must be accompanied by pleasant experiences with the spouse as lover. Giving up the expectation that a therapist will be a loving parent to oneself and harsh avenging judge to the frustrating spouse must be accompanied by increasing enjoyment of the therapist as an honest workman, a coach of relationships. A marital therapist encourages the interaction of fantasy and experience between spouses and with himself and each partner. Dreams and fantasy are driving forces that generate goals and hope, but they must be harnessed to possibilities in a limited world in order not to wither in despair.

IDENTIFYING AND REDUCING
SHARED STEREOTYPED PATTERNS

In Chapter 4, I presented the concept of spin-outs, the term used for the most dramatic of a couple's shared stereotyped interacting patterns. They are behavioral sequences that produce escalating alienation until some agreed-upon overwhelming factor or "brake" intervenes. The patterns are specific to the couple; they differ in content from one pair to the next. Examples:

Couple A presents with a spin-out pattern of *his* anxiety producing withdrawal from emotional encounters and immersion in his professional work, and *her* helpless frustration producing shrill emotional attacks on his competence. Each annoys the other in the usual escalation.

Couple B presents with *his* consistently trying to solve all problems by force—bullying his wife and tyrannizing their children. *She* continually appeases him, behaves ineptly, and experiences miserable confusion. Each reinforces the other's maladaptive pattern.

Couple C presents with *her* frustration producing attacks on his motives and trustworthiness as *he* stays away from home, physically withdrawing into work or extramarital activities.

These patterns are predictable; however, as weeks and months pass in treatment, the partners may reverse roles. *He* assumes *her* behavior and she his, and then they reverse once again. There are many good reasons for this. Ubiquitous ambivalence extends to rules and patterns.

For example, "borderline" characters have difficulty in keeping any constellation of thought and behavior well expressed or repressed, and are peculiarly subject to these oscillations. More developmentally capable and differentiated partners also oscillate, but usually more slowly. Also, an individual psyche is made up, in large part, of memories, roles and interacting patterns of the whole family of origin's constellation, so identification is never limited to one individual. Even in those unusual families with an isolated single parent raising a lonely, only offspring, at least two parts are learned.

Case Example. Mr. and Mrs. W. have had a painful conflicted marriage for 24 years. She has been erroneously diagnosed as schizophrenic by a previous therapist though she functions reasonably well as a housewife. She has fluctuating moods, intermittent rages, and periods of dramatic helplessness. He is a successful professional, usually cool and collected, who is easily goaded by his wife into hysterical rages and dramatic irrational behavior.

He has a psychotic sister and a doting but controlling mother. She comes from a control-oriented family in which there was seldom any spontaneous display of emotion. Each has multiple alternating roles in their tragic relationship.

Treatment is necessarily focused on shoring up boundaries, helping each define wishes and choices and stabilize self-definition. Resolution of individual ambivalence is necessary for resolving the marital conflict and oscillating role-playing.

There are some stereotyped patterns that are seen frequently in troubled couples. These include "playing to the referee," "building a case," the "unholy bargain," intimidation, and sexual stereotypes.

Playing to the Referee and Building a Case

No troubled couple that I have known has been free of the shared assumption that there is a "right" way to think, feel and act. The partners differ wildly, of course, on *what* is right. This firm, sometimes unshakeable belief in an ordered universe, with a cosmic referee heaping coals of fire on the heads of miscreants, produces a variety of painful, frightening, and cruel results. The referee appealed to is a family referee expected to be universal; he or she is powerful, capable of reward and punishment, the last word in judgment—much as a parent is seen by a three-year-old child.

Why do grown people assume the child's position in marital disharmony? Perhaps because love is the only area of life in which we expect to get a great deal without learning how to obtain it. Also, those of us who have had the most painful, pathetic family experiences are the most insistent that we have "suffered enough," that we should get from a lover what we missed out on at home. In other words, adults who have been taught the least interpersonal skills expect the most in a marriage. Further, this childlike orientation may well have been the level at which life in the family of origin was experienced. Many patients come to treatment with extraordinary social skills in business or social activities that dissipate like morning mist at the front door of home.

One behavior that results from the attitude that the cosmic referee exists, is "building a case." A picture for this is a person sitting on a limb in a high tree and sawing it off. "She is the world's worst cook and then will blame me for not complimenting her." "He doesn't know how to love; he is utterly self-centered." "She has no interest in my welfare." Even while spending time and money on how to live together enjoyably, they persist in making the extreme case that the other is impossible.

If the situation is that bad, any reasonable person would leave. Or, if circumstance or belief requires the marriage to continue, a prudent person would carefully negotiate an attempt to make a bad deal in some ways better. These courses of action make sense, unless there is some superhuman figure who, when properly appealed to, would punish the partner for being bad and enforce good behavior. This figure exists in the minds of the partners and is ready to be projected onto the therapist—or onto the spouse! I have had more than one patient confess sheepishly that he or she was aware of the desire to make it sound so bad that the partner would successfully argue to the contrary. This is an excellent and frightening example of caring and loving producing destructive behavior.

Blame is prominent in these scenes. "I am virtuous and she is bad." "My psychiatrist is better than your psychiatrist because he is warm and understanding; yours is acting out his countertransference." "I do everything I'm supposed to and you stay out late and ignore me."

The belief in a referee presupposes several false assumptions: that family rules are universal; that there are real adults out there somewhere who are bigger than my spouse and I; and that I am little in comparison to my spouse and to significant and valuable people in the outside world. The therapist will deal directly with all these and more, bringing to awareness the referee syndrome, along with the family rules embedded in each person's thinking. As each individual condemns the other and states the situation is impossible and cannot get better, this, too, is taken seriously.

She: "He doesn't love me or care anything about me."
Therapist: "I have a feeling that you are not sure of that or you wouldn't be such a fraud—to lead me and your husband on like this."
She: "Well, I don't see any evidence of it. Of course, I do hope that he does."
Therapist: "You want to ask him?"

The issue of little and big comes up repeatedly. There is a striking tendency for warring spouses to see each other as malevolent, stupid, and willful, but nevertheless possessing the wisdom to judge the intent and success or failure of the partner. The therapist may intervene: "You seem to have really mixed feelings about her, John." Or, "Okay, I will believe he's an unloving, selfish idiot if you insist, or that he is the big man, able to decide whether you are a good woman and a good wife, but I get dizzy trying to believe both at the same time." Or, "What would it take to feel that you are worthy of respect?"

It is necessary to clarify boundary problems in eliminating the referee routine, and I have several metaphors in helping people grasp the possibilities of judging themselves: "You seem to imagine yourself as a bit part player in your own movie. I would like for you to have star billing in your own movie, for goodness sakes!" Or, "You have my permission to drive your own bus, but right now it seems like you feel yourself to be a passenger in that bus." Or, "Here, take this baton; you may conduct your own orchestra. Don't give that baton up to anybody—not to me, not to your spouse. I promise, if you keep the baton, you will come across more lovable, not less."

The Unholy Bargain

Most disturbed couples make what I call the unholy bargain. This bargain is as follows: "You take one-half of my ambivalence and I'll take the other half of yours. Neither of us will experience an internal conflict and both of our anxiety levels will drop; our self-image will seem clearer. The only unfortunate side effect is that we will fight like hell for 40 years."

Projection, of course, is a vital part of this picture. It is often shared by partners in a symbiotic fashion.

He: "I would like to go out, but I feel lonely even in a crowd." This is a painful internal conflict.

She: "I would like to stay at home, but I believe there is a lot I'm missing." Again, a difficult internal struggle.

The pseudo solution:

He: "I like to go out, but she never wants to."

She: "He has no interests in our home. I have to stay home and do what must be done by myself."

Unwinding this requires a keen appreciation of the pervasive reality of ambivalent feelings and the claiming by both
sides of the ambivalence. Spotting behavior that puts the
lie to monolithic beliefs, we then have two confused people
on the same side sorting out how they would like to live
their lives.

Spouses usually desire divorce for the same reasons they
desired marriage. The same behavior patterns of the partner that attracted are those that are most apt to be attacked
in later years. I think this is because we tend to marry in an
effort to finesse the need for growing up! If I am shy, perhaps my outgoing lover can carry my social needs; if I am
always on stage, aggressive and histrionic, perhaps my quiet,
sensitive lover can feed the constant hunger within me. But
as years go by, it becomes apparent that the other person's
skills are not satisfying; marriage is no protection against
the requirement to grow up. AMEN!

It is frequently quite easy to get warring spouses on the
same side by suggesting that each can learn from the skills
of the other and both can become broader and more capable.
The therapist offers a problem-solving orientation focused
on present needs and solutions. Example:

She: "I have dinner ready every night at 6:30 and I never know
when he will be there. He never calls if he is late. He doesn't care
about me, and I'm fed up with living with uncertainty and rejec-
tion."
Therapist: "Okay. You want him more predictable. John, what
do you say about that situation?"
He: "Well, I'm tired of being controlled. She wants to know
every move I make and I can't take care of my business and check
in with her every 10 minutes."
Therapist: "So you want more flexibility. Do you also want enjoyable hot dinners or is that relatively unimportant to you?"

The idea here is to help the two negotiate a good deal for

both, with what is expected becoming clearer. No "proper" solution can be entertained, but only a solution that participants will claim as their own. Contradictory expectations then become obvious and ego skills improve. In this process family of origin issues emerge. For example, John realizes his fear of being controlled relates as much or more to his mother's behavior in his early years as to his wife's at the present time. Contrasting *then* (being a child, having particular family rules and unmet needs from parents) with *now* (being an adult, able to define new family rules and resolve conflicts with other equals) and practicing some *now* solutions works to reduce angry attacks and stalemates. As a rule, the process is clearer and invites greater cooperation when one first deals with practical issues and then with historical interferences with present solutions, such as John's wishing to be free and yet wanting the waiting hot dinner his mother always provided. Less obvious realities are dealt with only as direct solutions prove inadequate.

Intimidation

Attacks on the other by blaming are a way of direct intimidation resulting from the assumption of a referee. Intimidation by inducing either fear or guilt is unproductive because it produces an increasingly resistant partner. Even cooperation becomes wooden, lifeless and sullen, and outright opposition is an ever-present danger. With the expectation of a referee, intimidation seems the only way to get what one wants. Eliminating the belief in such a referee forces the partners to consider each other's perceptions; subjective reality becomes a central theme. Who am I married to? What does he or she really want? How many of our goals might become compatible? With the therapist continually reaching for each person's own truth and expressing his perceptions as only one person's reality, subject to and desperately needing others' contributions, a bit of magic usually occurs. Humor develops, bitterness dissolves, and the proceedings themselves become pleasurable rather than grim and frightening.

As people learn that their eye is not God's eye, that they cannot successfully appeal to another human as the final authority, there is a necessary and inevitable shift toward reaching out to both partner and therapist for support in common causes. A counterproductive oppositional assumption has been destroyed and ground has been broken for an affiliative relationship.

Blame indicates anger, of course, but also a moralizing mind-set. If the significance of the subjective view of reality seeps into a couple's transactions, blame is obsolete and can be replaced by honest exploration of differences.

She: "You never take me seriously; you always take me for granted, I haven't heard a kind word from you in weeks. You are so wrapped up in your business that you could care less."

He: "You see, doctor, she gets so emotional I can't do anything with her. I just leave her alone until she comes to her senses."

Each has an idea of what is proper behavior. *She* feels that people should express warmth and *he* feels that people should have self-discipline. Neither is yet curious as to why the other fails to meet these expectations which, though definite, are not explicit. When these expectations are made clear to all three, the "should" behind them becomes the focus. "You should be warm." "You should be unemotional." These are inept means of saying, "I feel alone and unloved." "I feel scared and picked on." Using the referee is a way of sounding big, of using authority, yet the naked expression of vulnerability and need is much more effective and can be learned.

Sexual Stereotypes

A healthy marital relationship encourages individual autonomy and responsibility. The family system that such a couple develops is not at odds with individual development; in fact, each requires the other. Male and female are not inevitably at odds, nor are the individual and the family group. Any assumption of inevitable conflict represents projections of the tension within an individual onto the larger group. These projections are encouraged by unchallenged sexual stereotypes. As assumptions are challenged and eliminated or made tentative, new learning can take place and new satisfactions can be obtained by broadening definitions of maleness and femaleness. Most fathers become delighted with parenting when given permission to do so. Mothers find new joy in children with a willing partner and/or excitement and interests beyond the home. Mike to Gloria Stivec

A current cultural myth describes the unfulfilled woman who goes back to school or work over the bigoted opposition of the husband who must take on more responsibilities and have less satisfaction from this new woman. Couples perceiving themselves in this oppositional bind have not properly dealt with the difficulties of being an individual in any social situation. Depressed women and distant husbands are often similar in their degree of pain or satisfaction. If she is able to define herself as a choice-making adult, he receives more from her. Or, if she sees him as the reason for her difficulty and *he* guiltily agrees or disagrees, the stage is set for projection, blame, and failure of resolution. In family tragedies, there are no villains, only victims, and a systems-oriented therapist can break down sexual stereotypes that encourage false myths and false solutions.

The meek and mild wife who accepts submission becomes depressed. Her husband tries to make her feel better and fails. In most treatment situations, she will go through what

I term a "Nat Turner" transition: From the kitchen galley slave she becomes an "angry free woman" who sees men as her enemy. This is a projection of her introjected bad image culturally encouraged and transmitted by the family. If needs, choices, and practical solutions are highlighted, her angry aggressiveness can become effective assertiveness. The husband's helpless guilt or rage can become a new appreciation of living with a verbal person rather than a compliant stranger. It is in this area of helping people emerge as individuals rather than sexual stereotypes that the therapist's bias may be reinforced by theoretical dogma; for example, some therapists would define this woman's anger as penis envy, and some "modern" feminist therapists would support her projection onto husband and men in general. Couples therapy reduces the probability of these destructive therapist attitudes, but the careful therapist will be concerned to remain the ombudsman of both partners, smoking out the hunger and wishes of each, and assisting each to define needs that are usually complementary.

Case Example. Mr. and Mrs. R. came into treatment at her insistence because of his preoccupation with work and uncommunicativeness. She was childlike in manner, but was capably working on an advanced professional degree. She soon let it slip that her effort to get more education was an attempt to hedge against a probable divorce, since she could not easily support her children with only a bachelor's degree. Since he wanted the marriage very much, he found her ambition threatening. After she expressed a great deal of anger toward him, citing his emotional distance and "selfishness," the therapist helped her modify the intensity of these attacks and to render them intelligible to her easily frightened husband. As she saw him vary in the degree of warmth or withdrawal depending on the level of her attacks, she began to believe that he was a feeling person and needed her. She continued her graduate work but no longer tied this effort to divorce. He, reassured, began to woo her and express enjoyment of her. Though beginning as male and female caricatures, through treatment they took form as complex individuals. They left with acceptance of their marriage as mutually advantageous.

BOUNDARIES

The development of boundaries between the self and other is an ongoing, unending process. The challenge of individual identity (or "reality-testing," or consensual validation) is inevitably related to the subjective, never certain, effort to determine what comes from inside, what from the outside. Couples are in a continuing dialogue. Am I oblivious or is he projecting? Am I perceptive or she unfairly attacked? And *no one can ever* say for sure what is real, which is why capable grown people often search for a magical referee to make rules and judgments absolute.

Boundary problems are most evident in severely disturbed families with their incoherence, unclear context, and frequent evasiveness. With these couples, a good therapist is alert to recognizing confusion as to who is thinking or feeling what. When confusion occurs, he or she deals with it quickly. Speaking for others is a frequent and jarring example of boundary problems.

Case Example. Mr. and Mrs. G. presented themselves as an unhappy but generally capable pair who had some insight into their problem and some ability to be separate. However, it soon became apparent that she spoke for him frequently: "He really was angry but he couldn't express it." "He was anxious about coming home today." The therapist tried to catch the speaking for the husband each time it occurred and to stop the proceedings and ask Mr. G. to speak for himself. In the eighth session, however, the therapist found himself saying, "Well, you see, Mr. G. is fearful about expressing needs . . . " and his voice trailed off as all three broke into laughter. The pair was handing its invasive style to the therapist rather than learning something different! Shared laughter provided a significant moment as the partners learned that they have a powerful, if destructive, pattern and the therapist needed help in helping them. Further, Mr. G. invited the invasive statements of others since he could then be innocent and not responsible. This flash of insight destroyed a continuing game of heavy aggressive wife imposing her will on floundering husband.

In the illustration above, as much as Mrs. G. wished her husband to be more expressive, she had felt compelled to punish him almost every time that he did so, for he never said it "right." He was always disappointing her, never saying what she fancied he should say. Since both accepted the absurd notion that loving means being what the other desires, they both believed that he was unloving. The therapist smoked out the underlying family expectation, which was found to be present in both their families of origin, and then called attention to her inability to encourage his expression until she became interested in what he had to say rather than expecting just what she wanted. Here in a nonpsychotic pair were many boundary problems found in psychotic people. She projected a fantasy onto him, he accepted it, using her as a referee and futilely tried to hide from her judgments; she interpreted his motives and feelings as negative when he was different, and he acquiesced. They both reportedly had mothers who were chronically dissatisfied with their husbands.

As boundary difficulties lessened, hope was rekindled and each partner began to experience new pleasure in the other. The therapist challenged projections repeatedly, with increasing success. She claimed her sense of inadequacy; he, his punitive conscience. This owning up to the previously projected allowed more spontaneity and joy, in contrast to the stereotyped repetitiveness of two people locked into a relationship with chronically blurred boundaries.

Boundary difficulties are found in all degrees of family and marital difficulty. In midrange families where obvious blurring of boundaries is absent, there is still an abiding effort of family members to control one another. The implicit motto is "Loving means controlling." And for every controller, there is a controlled, whose role is also seen as valuable. Example:

She: "You never do the hard part of being a parent. You let the kids get by with anything. I have to be the heavy and lower the boom on them both or they would be little gangsters."

He: "Well, of course I give them a break. With you coming on like a little Hitler, somebody has to care."

Therapist: "Do either of you see any value in the other's position?"

Here a common internal parental conflict—how strict, how lenient—is made falsely simple by the one-half/one-half projection and emotional control efforts. The therapist must find some chink in the armor plate of this collusion. One person will usually admit to occasional uncertainty, which allows, through time, the claiming of both kinds of feelings, conscious anxiety, and finally, the recognition that each person's perceptions can be valuable to the other *because each is flawed*. We need the imperfect eye of the other to help us see a little better; if perfect, the eye would be insufferable. After enough work, we can hear:

He: "I have been stepping in more when the kids get out of hand. Martha is right, the kids respect me more when I don't just sit there."

She: "It really is great to relax and let Harry handle them sometimes. He's right, you know, they really are decent kids and usually do okay."

With boundaries intact, cooperation is possible, as each individual claims what formerly had to be repressed. "Loving means controlling" can be replaced with "Loving means respecting what the other has and is."

Getting boundaries reasonably clear is necessary, satisfying, and sometimes difficult. When a shared projective game is going on in front of me, I find myself (sitting as I do, directly in front of the pair) splitting the air between them with my hand, hacking out some separateness between the two. A useful part of boundary treatment consists of interaction between therapist and each partner; new learning can occur through modeling if the therapist refuses to make it a bargain of shared projections, thus forming a new response.

A common projection to the therapist is, "You don't like me. You just like my wife (husband)." This calls for a stout restatement of a fundamental treatment bargain: "You don't tell me what I think (feel) and I don't tell you what you think (feel). You ask me, I'll ask you, and if either of us doesn't believe the answer we get, we will explore the information available to us both." Sometime I have to agree with a patient that I don't really like what he has been doing. This may lead to investigation of how obnoxious behavior can drive people away. At other times, the accusation, "You don't like me," just misses me totally and I insist on looking at whatever data the accusing person has.

This focus on the dignity and the significance of the internal living space in people, and on the pragmatic and the shareable, will wither the most persistent projective tendency. In the process, both partners learn—through the interaction and by direct observation—that a person does not have to cooperate with this process of being invaded, and that it can be resisted and overthrown.

HONESTY

Honesty is just *a* policy, not always the best policy even in intensely close relationships. We are always selecting, screening, and monitoring our communications and even our most "spontaneous" interchange; this is a necessary part of being a capable adult. Many couples enter treatment after a variety of therapists have blindly encouraged "openness" ("Express your true feelings"), which then comes to serve as an external referee. "You can't criticize me; I'm expressing how I feel."

Case Example. Mr. and Mrs. N. were referred for couples treatment following extensive individual and family therapy. Both were highly intelligent, complex and guarded. A statement from either brought forth a host of responses from the other. In 20 years of unfulfilling, unresolved, complicated, painful interaction, Mr. N. had learned a technique of directness that effectively seared his partner.

"I'm fantasing having an affair with my secretary, and I know she is willing and eager."

When Mrs. N. met such a statement with angry hurt, he would respond, "How can we get closer if we are not open with each other?"

I know of only one effective antidote to this virtuous sadism. That is the formula of asking oneself, "What am I trying to do? And how am I trying to do it?"

I used this with Mr. N. forcefully and developed the family rule that wishes, desires, and responsibility must reside within the same person. One cannot make another responsible for one's goals. That is not a moral statement, but a technical one—it simply does not work. Gradually, Mr. N. came to see that he was treating his wife in a manner more appropriate to his mother—expecting her, rather than himself, to be responsible for his fantasy life, a role that neither she nor any other woman could fulfill. Since he had had numerous affairs in previous years, he could only improve their level of trust by becoming responsible for his statements and their impact. His childlike honesty was not helpful. Decent boundaries necessarily include this acceptance of responsibility for the results of any actions, verbal or behavioral.

AUTONOMY AND CHOICE

With boundaries shored up and relatively clear, the satisfying experience of personal choice is possible. There are many sane people who have never experienced the satisfaction of individual choice in any significant area of life! Every decision can be ascribed to authority, relatives, spouses or children, and in this way an unholy bargain with the cosmos is maintained: I will be responsible for nothing, I will control no aspect of my life, and therefore I am blameless.

These people believe in the mischievous concept that an individual and a group are in eternal opposition and have essentially conflicting advantages. In therapy, this concept must be challenged vigorously and repeatedly. There is *tension* between being a woman and a mother or wife, between being a man and a father or husband, but there need not be a continual, frustrating, oppositional struggle. A person is nobody except as he or she makes decisions to commit to ideas, roles, activities, and people. An individual is known by choices and commitment, which express personhood. Disturbed families perpetuate an assumed dichotomy between person and families; it is important that therapists know better.

Families vary in competence directly with the ability of family members to resolve ambivalence and to make choices. With ambivalence resolved, conflict is truly, not falsely, moved to the interpersonal arena, and conflict resolution becomes the responsibility of the family unit. Since conflict resolution is possible only after individuals have taken responsibility for their feelings and choices, when one family member makes up his or her mind, then even heated family conflict can be resolved effectively. What I have termed "vectoring"—resolving ambivalence and moving in a coherent direction with power and force—is necessary for capable family functioning. This relationship is most important; they are not at odds, but depend upon each other. Family systems do not change automatically; therapists and family members change systems.

DE-FANGING THE "SHOULDS"

A frequent enemy of resolving individual and couple conflicts is the "should"—the voice of the inhuman, all-powerful referee defining what people should do, with no regard for their own dignity, wishes or perceptions.

>   He: "I should be a better father, but I never have time."
>   She: "I should stop smoking and lose weight, but I'm always so nervous and needful."
>   Or he: "You should stop smoking and lose weight."
>   Or she: "You should become a decent father."

There are several remedies to this fruitless pattern, and all are designed to replace the referee with a human and practical rule system. From, "What should I do?" it becomes, "What do I want to do and how do I accomplish it?" These remedies include "finishing the sentence" and "according to whom".

"Finishing the sentence" refers to the simple process of completing these "should" sentences. "I should be a better father," becomes an item on an adult's agenda if a goal is defined: "if I'm going to be much of an influence on my children's lives," or, "if I'm going to enjoy the children." "I should lose weight" is an oppressive, usually counterproductive statement of guilt. With a goal such as, "if I want to be more attractive," or, "if I want to play tennis like I used to," it becomes an entry into decision-making.

"According to whom" is a way of bringing in the power of subjective reality, the idea that no human has a corner on the truth. Example:

She: "He has no right to go off on these business trips week after week when I am here all alone."

Therapist: "According to whom?"

She: "Well, don't you think that is terrible, leaving me all alone with the kids?"

Therapist: "Am I the judge, in your mind? If so, I pass. I'm trying to get you and your spouse to agree on some rules and I'll never do that by offering my own knotheaded ideas about how you should live your life. Can you tell him how you feel about his business trips?"

She: "Well, I hate them. I can't stand them. I want him at home where he should be."

Therapist: "Should? According to whom?"

She: "Oh, you are starting that again. Okay—I just don't like it."

Therapist: "How do you feel, Tom, about what she just said?"

He: "Well, I have to make a living and I am a salesman; she knew that when we got married. She is always trying to make me do what she wants."

Therapist: "Didn't you say that you had been offered a desk job and turned it down recently?"

He: "Yes, and it did pay better, but only temporarily. I think I can increase my income by selling more."

Therapist: "Uh-huh, but you have the capacity for deciding whether you stay at home or stay on the road?"

He: "Sure, if I wanted to cut off the chances for commission profit."

Therapist: "So, you see yourself in a quandary, possibly losing money or having an angry wife."

He: "Yes, and I'm damned resentful of that bind. How come she can't help me and support me like any decent wife should?"

Therapist: "According to whom?"

No magic, but encouragement of partners to understand the limits of subjective reality and the hollowness of trying to force a non-negotiable absolute.

POWER AND INTIMACY

Equal relationship power is necessary for intimacy between marital partners. This equality of power must be experienced by both or it does not exist. A blatant example from individual therapy is the patient in the throes of transference who sees the therapist as an all-powerful parent. Though the therapist may perceive the patient as worthy of respect and dignity, as sovereign in his life as the therapist is in his own, it makes no difference operationally until both people accept this viewpoint. Similarly with couples, the experiencing of intimacy, the sharing of the innermost with another, is an unending hunger, but perceived power differences provide an atmosphere of anxiety and fear that precludes openness and sharing.

Most members of troubled couples not only frequently view their partners as more powerful, much as a parent to a small child, but also attempt to obtain objectives through intimidation—the purposeful effort to make an overt power difference. Shaming, direct angry attacks, and judgmental "shoulds" are direct ways of intimidating. Becoming nonfunctional, irrational, childlike or suicidal is a reverse way of intimidating. (There is a cartoon that illustrates this reversal: A battered boxer comes to his second between rounds and says, "I've got him where I want him—he's afraid he's going to kill me!")

To be effective, the therapist must help the couple to experience equal transactions that allow for mutual dignity and respect and to gain new satisfactions from these skills. The methods for performing this task vary, and the styles of intervention vary, but there are several required elements in the treatment situation. These include experiential learning of the desired transactional patterns, inviting and modeling an equal-powered relationship by the therapist, and a sample within the treatment situation of the gratification to be had via shared power with shared respect and dignity.

Troubled couples come from a variety of dysfunctional families of origin, and many individuals who are not obviously disturbed appear never to have experienced an equal relationship! Obviously, if this is the case, insight will be of little help and experiential learning looms large as the instrument of change.

NEUROTIC GUILT AND "MASOCHISM"

The continuing attacks that go on between troubled spouses are often due to the neurotic guilt of each partner, which makes most difficult their acceptance of various aspects of being human. A person can take responsibility without blaming others for life's tragedies only if there is reasonable self-acceptance and a relative lack of neurotic guilt.

Neurotic guilt is to be distinguished from useful guilt: A rule of thumb is that "good guilt" produces behavioral change and does not last more than five minutes. "Bad" or neurotic guilt often promotes unacceptable behavior and is a source of continuing emotional pain. I have observed that many people will clutch their painful guilt *in order to feel powerful!* They have been taught that being in control is important, and therefore feeling guilty is reassuring since they can believe that they are messing up rather than that they are vulnerable, needful, frightened and unable to control a situation.

A simple and frequent clinical example of this is the person who says, "I want a divorce, but my wife (husband) could not handle it, so I must continue this joyless, loveless farce. I could never forgive myself if I left him/her, and even feel guilty about thinking of leaving." Explored by a therapist, this guilt is usually covering fear: "Will I do well as a divorced person?" The therapist can proceed to make the guilt-prone person get sick of, even laugh at, this powerful posturing. I tell patients I want to make them guilty about being guilty; that is, I want them to identify the neurotic guilt, with its ugly tendency to keep people in a stuck position, and to observe its fraudulence. Then good guilt can emerge with the realization: I am a scared, vulnerable human. I have a hard time making up my mind. When I see myself as guilty and powerful, I lose both choice and enjoyment.

One of the most dramatic evidences of a defect in autonomy, or a failure of choice, is behavior often termed "masochistic," behavior that appears to be self-defeating and self-punishing. The perseveration of such activities in patients is the bane of therapists of all persuasions. A simple way of understanding the origins of these frustrating patterns is suggested by a story.

A lumberjack lived in a boarding house and retired at 10 p.m. every evening. At 12 midnight, the huge laborer who lived upstairs always dropped his heavy shoe as he prepared for bed, which woke up our lumberjack. The laborer then smoked a cigarette and, at 12:15, dropped his other cumbersome shoe; then our man could return to sleep. This pattern continued unchanging for months. Then one night the first shoe hit the floor at 12:00, but 12:15, 12:20, 12:45, went by silently. Anxiety clutched the lumberjack; at 1:30 he could stand it no longer and ran upstairs in his nightshirt shouting, "DROP THE OTHER SHOE!"

Just so, many patients have experienced frustrating family patterns and have assumed them to be inevitable. If by chance they experience something different, and frustration is replaced by enjoyment, respect, and love, then anxiety begins to mount. Thwarting a good time is less painful than the anxiety, which inevitably progresses to dread. It is not enough to change a couple's pattern of response to one another; there must also be an expectation that the more satisfying pattern can continue. Telling the "other shoe" story is one of my ways of bringing to awareness the fact that one's own history can cause one to sabotage present possibilities. This helps marital partners to believe they can indeed influence a spouse to become more rewarding on a predictable and trustworthy basis.

Learning to recognize that I can influence others, but not control them absolutely, that I can move in a direction of my choice but have limits that require me to attend others' wishes, is to develop a systems orientation, a necessary part of individual autonomy. The capacity to negotiate depends on such a systems orientation. I can make my wishes known to you, but I must consider your perceptions, needs, and fears if I hope to gratify my own desires. With this approach, selfishness becomes valuable, not threatening. Most spouses come into treatment with "You're selfish!" as a ready epithet for the other. I immediately seize such a moment to say, "Oh, I hope so!" and embellish that remark if needed with others, such as "I can treat anybody who is selfish. I can't do anything with someone who is unselfish." "If you will pursue your own wishes, I guarantee that you will be more lovable."

SUMMARY

Common problems in treating chronic marital dissatisfaction include contextual and contractual difficulties, communicational confusion, shared stereotyped patterns, boundary problems, and problems in resolving ambivalence and in making choices. Practical means of handling these frequently encountered emotional difficulties are presented, with the overall goals of improving negotiating ability and shared satisfactions.

There is no way that a couple or a family can encourage individual autonomy unless human drives are seen as neutral or benign, and this requires clients and therapists to dismiss such ominous concepts as basic malevolence or masochistic drives. When a lively attention to self-interest is seen as a necessary prior condition to enjoying relationships, and this self-interest is understood as a legacy of being human and of having been a child, neurotic guilt is lessened and individual choice becomes a respectable goal.

8 APPROACHING FAMILIES OF ORIGIN FROM A SYSTEMS PERSPECTIVE

Families, like individuals, have a kind of "script"; they have a beginning and a developmental course, although the end is always in question. Are Darwin's ideas dead? Does any family totally disappear?

In former times, physicians of the mind tracked the life history of their patients. Neurologists and alienists were intensely, sometimes feverishly, interested in the natural history of mental disease. They did not expect themselves to do anything particularly remarkable; their expertise lay in *knowing* the multiple and subtle evidences of syndromes. Freud was to these spectator experts something of a spoilsport because he tried to intervene, to change things, to transmute neurotic illness into common unhappiness. He became a highly visible missionary to the mind. By today's standards, however, his therapy seems slow and cautious. With ever more driven and desperate optimism, legions of mental health professionals have pursued active interventionist techniques.

These two approaches to emotional problems or illness—a data-gathering, educational (anthropological) approach and an energetic, fix-it (missionary) approach—have alternated in prominence in the mental health field for close to 100 years. Each has been associated with power and abuse. In the 1920s, for example, when the autointoxication theory of madness was widely accepted, the colons of suffering schiz-

ophrenics were removed in an effort to cure their illness.
The results, when dispassionately evaluated, were psychotic
people with no colons, a pitiful failure of the well-meaning
intervention (21). In the last 70 years or so the Freudian missionary approach has been attenuated so that it has become
much closer to the anthropological approach—observe, re-
cord, comment, and report. On the other hand, with some
disorders (for example, anorexia nervosa), there is considerable evidence that active therapeutic intervention is much
more effective than a reflective stance (39).

The psychotherapist of the late 20th century is inevitably
dealing with the tension of these polar positions. There are
simultaneous directives to be active and to be passive, to fix
it and to understand it. The dual themes are found in psychoanalytic arguments, such as that between Kohut (35),
with his emphasis on the need for real human interchange
in treatment, and the orthodox Freudians (27), who still emphasize the non-real or transference issues. They are present in controversies between family therapy, usually a more
active orientation, and individual therapy. These themes are
also found in family therapy; for example, contrast Haley's
(31) belief in the therapist's responsibility for family change
with Boszormenyi-Nagy's focus on each family member's
responsibility (18).

At a different level, families who seek treatment face the
same dilemma. Is there a quick fix for emotional pain, pre-
packaged and bought off the shelf? Or is it necessary to
know one's family history, the ethnic and cultural roots, and
the ways in which the style and tempo of the present family
is tied to past generations of family systems, beliefs and attitudes? This dilemma is highly significant, yet it is frequently not made explicit by therapists or patients. In the powerful
interchange between family and therapist, health or normali-
ty may be defined according to a particular style, or the complex history and patterns of both the husband's family and

the wife's family may be utilized to determine the path to success in family developmental tasks.

Intervention with couples is sometimes quite active and sometimes reflective. One approach takes the form of a partnership between couple and therapist, with the couple encouraged to develop the anthropological approach and avoid being missionaries to their families of origin. An activist approach to the family of origin has been well delineated (2). This consists of a presumably enlightened family member seeking out relatives and aggressively attempting to alter their habitual behavior patterns to something the activist believes healthier. In contrast, I will present a method of helping families to learn the rules, processes and patterns of their families of origin and to utilize this information to firm up the current family identity. Choices will be made: this to keep, this to modify, this to avoid. But there will be no attempt to change the family of origin except by example or in response to any request for help. Couples can, by becoming experts on their own origins, develop a practical systems orientation—your family, my family, our family. The result is elevated awareness of previously unnoticed family processes. With greater awareness comes increased choices and wider choices, as well as increased possibilities for negotiation.

METHODS USED IN THE SYSTEMS APPROACH

There are probably an infinite number of ways for this anthropological/systems approach to be taught and learned; I use the following:

1) *Eyewitness accounts*: Verbal descriptions of the family of origin, with free-for-all kibitzing by spouses and/or children.
2) *Field trips*: Visiting a family of origin with the directed goal

of studying together, observing, and finding time to compare notes.

3) *Inviting the natives to tea*: Utilizing visits from a family of origin, observing how family members interact with each other and with the current family and how the systems impact one another.

4) *Case studies*: Inviting parents or siblings of the couple involved in treatment to attend a session.

5) *Data analysis*: Integrating these various ways of observing how families interact and sharing conclusions about goals, processes, and rules for the present family.

I will take each of these methods in turn and describe how they are accomplished.

Eyewitness Accounts

Couples provide verbal descriptions of their families of origin. Even in the first interview, there is usually an opportunity to inquire of each spouse as to how his or her growing-up experience influences present behavior. If one partner falters, the spouse will usually be more than happy to offer suggestions.

Case Example. Mr. and Mrs. X., ages 32 and 33, had come to a children's clinic because of their seven-year-old son's behavior problems, but they soon agreed that their marriage was in more trouble than he was. Mrs. X. thought she wanted out, perceiving Mr. X. as sexually uninteresting, emotionally distant and intolerably sloppy. Mr. X., in turn, spoke of his desire to continue the marriage, even though his wife seemed to him constantly depressed, driven, controlling and joyless. In the first couples interview, Mr. X. volunteered that his distancing was related to his family experience, where both mother and father drank heavily and were frequently physically abusive to each other and to him and his siblings. Mrs. X. recalled that her parents also drank heavily, but in her family tremendous efforts at control, rather than physical abuse, determined the atmosphere. Meals were exactly at six, everything was tidy, and there were devastating verbal attacks on anyone who faltered.

Mrs. X. remembered liking Mr. X. because he was comfortable to be around and made her more confident in social situations. He recalled that she helped him stabilize and become more responsible, though this had been a gradual process over several years.

Rather quickly, several things became apparent to couple and therapist. Each spouse had initially described all of the marital faults that existed in the other, but as they began to talk of their upbringing, each could more easily accept that some of his or her own long-standing difficulties and maladaptive behavior contributed to their dreary stuck marriage. Already the awareness of a systems orientation was dawning. From "the problem is you," the discussion moved to, "The problem is ours," and, "We each missed something growing up." Further, they could get a glimmer of an important fact: that people usually want to divorce for the same reasons that they wanted to get married. In this instance, Mrs. X. loved Mr. X. partly because of his "laid back" attitude, which made her feel accepted, and yet she attacked him because he was not more structured. Mr. X., on the other hand, loved Mrs. X. partly because she could make him want to be responsible, but he was frustrated and angry at her criticism of his sloppy ways and her lack of desire to have fun.

With more work, both could see that their families of origin had some strengths, values and traditions that were quite worthy of respect. Mrs. X.'s parents were responsible even under stress; Mr. X's parents gave the children room and freedom. In the process of looking at these three families (the present one and that of each spouse), the familiar victim, persecutor, and rescuer triad was abandoned and replaced with an appreciation for mixed feelings, mixed virtues, and mixed evils. Mr. and Mrs. X. were able to move from the judgmental to the evaluative in remembering and observing their families. Inevitably they softened the judgmental stance with each other, moving toward trying to understand rather than futilely attempting to change each other. Of course, from this more open approach, negotiation was more successful and change did occur.

Field Trips

Sometimes I ask couples in treatment to make field trips, to visit the family of origin with the goal of studying, observing, and comparing notes. Every couple develops family rules and patterns which will inevitably be different from those of either spouse's family. These rules and patterns may be unclear and undefined or, as a result of discussion and negotiation, relatively clear and often explicit (6).

Rules may be a continuing source of marital conflict or, when both spouses perceive themselves as having improved on the families they came from, a basis for pride and cohesiveness. Particularly when one or both partners have been in treatment, there may be a persistent effort on the part of these grown children to become uninvited missionaries, attempting to change their parents' way of operating and thus bring enlightenment to a family that has been functioning for 25 years or more. From my clinical perspective the results of this missionary approach are uniformly poor. When the couple tries to change the family of origin of one spouse, conflicts between generations are heightened, not resolved. Hurt feelings multiply and the visit becomes a nightmare. Holiday times come to be dreaded (though perhaps occasionally anticipated with grim relish at the prospect of trying once more to convert the heathen).

When I have worked with a couple for at least several sessions, and a parental visit is planned, I call attention to the defects of the missionary approach (not position!) and suggest the value of relative ease of an anthropological orientation. Here is their opportunity to learn firsthand the rules of the game of the family from whence one partner came. If the belief is, for example, that Mother is terribly controlling, how does Mother control and what does Father do when she makes her moves? What does she obtain for herself in this habitual pattern? What are the advantages to Father? If there are children from the family of origin still in the home, how does each child interact in the parents' predictable "dance"?

So much data can be obtained in a short time with this approach! The couple learns that control is reciprocal; loud talking is countered with silence, intimidation defeated by helplessness, needs met in unexpected ways. The natives with their strange customs have managed to survive for many years, and the observer who does not judge too quickly will develop respect for these survival strategies.

I caution the couple working with me to take care that neither is "cut from the pack." It is perilous to go into a strange culture alone: One either "goes native" or is seen as quite weird. The couple needs to arrange time alone together, to talk about what they have learned, to regroup and get back together, so the learning can continue.

The spouse whose family is being visited will understandably tend to fall back into the role dictated in years past. (In fact, this may be the principal reason for the missionary approach; the fear of sliding back can produce the intense effort to convert.) Such a tendency, if predicted and expected, can be successfully avoided by frequent touching base with the spouse not so ingrained with the family history.

Case Example. Mr. and Mrs. N. had come into treatment because their 11-year-old daughter was a behavior problem at school and at home. Mr. N. came from a family that did everything right. They were honest, upright, conventional, as was Mr. N. Mrs. N., in contrast, had had a painful early life. Her mother had divorced when she was 10; then her stepfather, who entered the picture when she was 12, had sexually molested her from age 12 to age 17, when she left home to make a life for herself. She was never able to make her mother believe that the stepfather was abusing her. Mr. and Mrs. N. had both agreed that his family was great and hers was lousy.

A visit to his family was planned, and the anthropologist approach was recommended. After the week's visit, Mr. N. came back saying his family might be virtuous, but it sure was *dull*. Everything was so controlled, so predictable. He noted how each person in his family seemed to dampen any spontaneity in the others, with the result that he was newly appreciative of his wife's vivacity and occasional unpredictability. The next step was to arrange for a visit with her mother and stepfather, to see how this family could have produced such a delightful and interesting woman as Mrs. N. Following this visit, they were asked to make a list of the factors noticed in her family that were different from his but which seemed to have contributed to Mrs. N.'s strengths.

In this way, their own destructive mythology was successfully challenged. Mrs. N. held her head higher and stopped ruminating about her bad stepfather. The troubling black and white picture of "back street girl" and "white knight," which had contributed to so much covert conflict, metamorphosed into a multicolored picture of varying, frequently spontaneous spouses who approached joint decision-making from an equal position. In this process, the daughter's difficulties faded into insignificance, since she was no longer carrying the burden of expressing the family conflict.

Visiting both families became more fun. (Anthropologists are not prevented from loving their natives just because they study them; quite the contrary, respect for people's values and beliefs is a vital part of loving.) Mrs. N. really tried to understand why her mother had stayed with the stepfather, seemingly oblivious to Mrs. N.'s efforts to communicate her problems with the stepfather's sexual advances. She could empathize with the plight of a divorced woman with three children and no job skills, and observed that sometimes adaptation may include behavior that is not "by the book"—at least not by an etiquette book. This, in turn, helped her forgive herself for the enjoyment she remembered from the sexual molestation, for, along with disgust, fear, apprehension, and anger, there had also been pleasure. This was a secret she had to keep even from herself until she understood and forgave her mother. In the process, her adamant hatred of stepfather abated.

Having accepted the possibility of improving relationships with the families of origin by assuming the anthropological stance, couples may still fear the judgmental fire and brimstone that some parents can rain down on spouses and their children. Parents also try to be family missionaries, their attempts to convert taking the form of harsh condemnations of the choice of a partner, criticisms of childrearing methods, or attempts to influence decisions to divorce or not to divorce. Buckling under attacks such as these, taking on the rules of the tribe and giving up one's own, is the risk of "going native." I prepare couples and provide some tools for avoiding this kind of regression or loss of identity. The tools include: 1) staying in touch with each other; 2) avoiding triangles; 3) taking time-outs; 4) declaring oneself; 5) asking questions.

Staying in touch with each other. The current family's rules are most likely to be preserved when spouses are attuned to each other. Children sense when the rules are "up for grabs" while visiting their grandparents and will shamelessly use Grandma or Grandpa as a lever to get a short-term advantage. Grandma or Grandpa may equally shamelessly circumvent their child (the parent) regarding diet, sleep patterns and the like. It is only as spouses work together that they can maintain the fabric of their personal and family identity. Attacks from parents regarding choices of spouse, childrearing techniques, lovableness or loyalty can best be resisted with the support of a dependable partner. When single parents visit their own parents, I recommend taking a companion, spending time with a good friend in the town or city visited, or making very short visits. All alone, it is hard to resist the power of another family system for very long.

Avoiding triangles. Families of origin may have rules that include regular triangulation. One part of the triangle may be buffeted from both sides or may manipulate the other two sides by keeping them apart. I direct couples to watch for such triangulations in an anthropological manner and never try to reform when others—not the couple—are involved. Many families survive quite well with techniques that offend a systems sophisticate; changing them would require two things that are missing—motivation from the family members involved and motivation from the child-become-adult to handle all the repercussions that inevitably occur with growth-oriented changes.

But one must get oneself and one's spouse out of triangles. Does Dad get daughter off in the corner and complain about Mother? Does Mom get son-in-law in the kitchen and subtly suggest that he must have to put up with a lot? My recommendations to the couple are to back out, rejoin the group, cry for spouse, get a coughing fit, *but don't play.* Does Dad suggest that daughter Suzie always had a way with her brother Tom, and would she just talk with him a little about that woman he's running around with? A firm (not necessarily hostile) refusal and a flattering suggestion that Dad underrates his abilities may be called for. Practice time in treatment sessions is useful. The playing back and forth of identifying triangles and blocking them in the present family and in the family of origin sharpens systems skills and encourages the high morale associated with successful teams. Couples can then visit in-laws with the anticipation of holding their own rather than converting or submitting.

Taking time-outs. A successful visit of one family to another requires time to withdraw, to regroup, to share perceptions and redefine family boundaries. A parent in one family is a child in the other; the time-out allows for maintaining or reinstituting the sense of being adult and having a partner, not a parent. When the couple reports back in treatment session, these time-outs can be most useful in determining how successful the effort to stay in touch and avoid triangles has been. Walks, taking in a movie, visiting friends, letting grandparents take the children on outings while the couple stays home—all are simple and practical ways to maintain present family rules.

Declaring oneself. Electing to be anthropologists/systems observers does not exempt people from the responsibility of being human. Being clear about choices, risks and needs should not be confused with being judgmental or tyrannically imposing one family's rules on another.

Case Example. Mr. and Mrs. F. had been in couples treatment and intermittent family treatment with their two daughters, ages eight and 10, for about six months, primarily because of marital conflict and occasionally because of concern with one or the other daughter's behavior. Mrs. F. had described herself as attempting, during the early years of marriage, to be whatever her husband desired. In the last three years, however, she had been angry and depressed, grasping for some identity separate from her husband. Mr. F. agreed with this summary but stated that he had trouble either expressing or accepting anger and was most uncertain as to how to deal with Mrs. F.

Mrs. F.'s father had died some years previously and her mother had remarried. Mrs. F. had always felt understood and supported by her father, but she and her mother had always clashed. Her mother was perceived as insensitive, controlling and demanding, producing in Mrs. F. alternating rage and guilt.

The family planned a week-long return to their roots in another state, which entailed a visit to Mrs. F.'s mother and stepfather. We discussed in detail the approach and tools previously described. A special concern involved where they would stay. On previous trips Mrs. F.'s mother had insisted on their being at her house;

this time Mrs. F. wanted to be in a nearby motel so she could have some breathing room. The therapist and Mr. F. supported her in this desire, and the F. family did indeed stay in a motel during the visit. Mrs. F.'s mother was terribly "hurt"; she suggested that her daughter didn't love her, attempting a pretty good job of intimidating but to no avail. Mrs. F. did not get hysterical and did not lash out, as was her previous pattern, but simply stated her wish and, with her husband's help, followed through.

This event produced several significant changes. Mrs. F. was much less childlike—being neither compliant or rebellious, but rather more definite and clear—with her mother, stepfather, husband, and therapist. Mrs. F.'s mother reportedly began to talk to her as an adult, with some consideration of her opinions and wishes.

Practice sessions before the visit had focused on a non-defensive, non-attacking posture, and much was learned about boundaries, resolution of ambivalence, and the importance of choosing and being clear about choices.

Asking questions. Another method of resisting guilt induction or moralistic attacks is to ask questions. This is a time-honored maneuver of therapists; it should be shared with patients! When a parent is bearing down on what one does wrong, a careful investigation of his or her perceptions and alternative plan of action usually keeps the situation under control. If the attack is accompanied by clear advice (for example, "You need to make that child continue her music lessons"), questions as to when the speaker has used the technique, with whom, and what were the results, usually dilute unpleasant either/or situations into (at worst) tedious discussion. Occasionally, they provide opportunity for real understanding.

Inviting the Natives to Tea

This method uses visits from a family of origin to observe how the systems interact. When one spouse's parents (or whole family, for that matter) visits the couple's home, there is a marvelous opportunity to extend the anthropological approach to include *probes*. Family therapists use probes routinely, of course, to determine the family's adaptive capacity, characteristic patterns, and response to novelty. With coaching, the family in treatment can do just as well. Being on one's own turf is the key to the success of this additional tool. For example, several of my patients' families have found that the sternly non-drinking parents of one spouse accepted easily and without question the couple's offering choices of beverages, including cocktails, before dinner. These same parents would have been outraged had the couple brought liquor with them on a visit. Before trying the above described probe, many couples are convinced that Mom and Dad will self-destruct, commit mayhem or do some other dire or unclear thing if presented with any other family pattern. It is not possible to determine the degree of family adaptability until the family is presented with a novel choice.

Case Example. Mr. and Mrs. O. had been married several years before they had a child. In the midst of their joy over their new baby, John, they experienced the pain of learning that he had a rare metabolic disturbance which could affect his intellectual and emotional development. They subsequently had an umblemished child, Sophie, but continued to be preoccupied with John's development and adjustment problems and necessarily consulted many medical and mental health experts. Whenever they visited Mrs. O.'s parents (who lived in the same city), the program of parenting John, which had been carefully worked out with these various professionals, was effectively destroyed. Mrs. O.'s father and mother would tenaciously offer John anything his heart desired while almost ignoring Sophie.

I coached Mr. and Mrs. O. in making very short (one- or two-hour) visits to her parents and using the children (especially John) as "bait," inviting the grandparents to the O. home, and making the family rules stick. The grandparents were invited to assist the O.'s in helping John do well, with the method clearly outlined. As the grandparents accepted the O. family rules, soon longer visits could be made to the grandparents when it was desired by all concerned.

This exercise provided a fine opportunity for Mr. and Mrs. O. together to learn many systems concepts and strategies and allowed them to be closer to, rather than alienated from, her parents.

Case Studies

Sometimes it is helpful to invite parents and/or siblings to attend treatment sessions. Most of the couples I treat are transplants; that is, they were reared in other places and have migrated to this city, an expanding sunbelt metropolis. It follows that most of the families of origin live elsewhere and could not make regular visits to my office even if it were deemed valuable. However, their occasional visits are always educational, usually enjoyable, and sometimes pivotal in inducing useful change.

Case Example. Mr. and Mrs. F., mentioned earlier (see p. 200), invited Mrs. F.'s mother into the sessions. Before, Mrs. F. had merely reported her interaction with mother; now she was living it in the company of the therapist. Somehow, in this setting, she found it easier to view her mother as quite anxious, doubtful of her own lovableness, and desperately masking these unpleasant feelings by intermittent attacks on her daughter. Mrs. F. could even identify some of her mother's behavior in herself, and, since she was no longer so certain of its being malevolent, was able to forgive herself as well as her mother.

Case Example. Mr. and Mrs. Y. were locked in a well-bred but endless struggle for control; consequently, they frequently forgot to look for any pleasure in each other, in life, or in their children. As the therapist, my frequent approach in such intense battles is to ask (at what I hope are strategic times), ''What are you trying to do? *Right now*, what are you trying to do and how are you trying to do it?'' This usually gets the focus more clearly on gratification rather than on control, and negotiation proceeds.

In the Y.'s case, however, we got some unexpected help. Mr. Y. asked his parents to come into the session while they were visiting from another state, more because of the parents' curiosity than because of any current trouble. In the course of the interview, Mr. Y.'s mother told of the death of Mr. Y.'s brother and of his becoming anorectic soon after, at the age of five. The account of these events (which had been totally repressed by Mr. Y.) provided for all of us a sharply increased awareness of emotional hunger, denial, loss, and efforts at control that had influenced the couple's relationship patterns.

USING THE INFORMATION

These various ways of understanding family functions and processes are integrated and the conclusions are shared during the therapy. Therapists and couples can use a family of origin as a powerful force in efforts to understand family processes and can employ that knowledge to increase the skills, enjoyments, and competence of family members in treatment. The approach is not a quick fix to family difficulties, though it often can produce resolution to long-standing marital conflict.

9 SPECIAL CONSIDERATIONS IN MARITAL THERAPY

Previous chapters have presented theory, data, concepts, and clinical material about marital therapy in a generic fashion. We have been dealing with the human condition and the therapist's efforts to help people accommodate their needs to those of others in marital partnership. In this chapter, we deal with particular kinds of couples and particular issues that arise in marital therapy.

Let us begin with a clear look at couples that come from severely dysfunctional, borderline, and midrange families. The phrase "come from" is ambiguous: It could refer to either an individual's family of origin or to the current family that the two partners have developed. This term is, therefore, sufficiently vague and comprehensive for my purposes. Much of the time, these meanings (that is, family of origin and current family) coalesce. People from severely dysfunctional families have a way of choosing each other to marry, and people from borderline or midrange families also find each other. This occurs, in my opinion, because individual humans are comfortable with the familiar and are uncomfortable with people who have markedly different family rules in their heads and their behavior. Two strong predictions in marital treatment are 1) that partners have similar I.Q.'s, even though the family myth may be that one is "dumb" and one is "smart," and 2) that they come from families, regardless of stylistic differences, with about the same degree of distancing, trust and toleration of intimacy.

These observations support the somewhat mechanistic concept of systems therapy that automatically casts doubts on the possibility that one member of a couple may be very sick and the other well. My experience tells me that people marry partners who have similar family rules regarding distancing and intimacy.

It would follow, then, that individuals from severely dysfunctional families or midrange families would choose partners from similarly functioning families and set up households that are similar to these families of origin in particular ways, especially regarding interpersonal boundaries. There are exceptions, of course; some people escape from severely dysfunctional families, then find lovers who have done the same, and by tremendous effort, love, and luck develop a family rule system superior to what either of them knew as children. When a therapist finds such an unusual situation, he can congratulate the pair and suggest that this movement prior to entering treatment portends great possibilities for future adaptability.

Though one observes most human problems to some degree in every couple, clusters of particular problems and particular solutions are found in couples from the various levels of family functioning.

COUPLES FROM SEVERELY DYSFUNCTIONAL FAMILIES

This group represents about 20 percent of the couples referred to my private practice. Though some agencies will, of necessity, specialize in treating severely dysfunctional individuals or families, this group provides few couples who will continue treatment together over many sessions. With these couples, coherence and hope are the primary deficiencies. They are enmeshed in relationships where everyone seems to lose; nobody is gratified, choice is nonexistent, and unresolved ambivalence is rife, though vigorously denied.

— Mom

Severely dysfunctional centrifugal families deny the need for warmth and the desire to be close; severely dysfunctional centripetal families deny anger and the desire for separation. I will describe the specifics of work with couples from severely dysfunctional centripetal families, since I have had more experience with these couples than with couples from severely dysfunctional centrifugal families, where marital problems are more often dealt with by desertion or divorce.

To dysfunctional centripetal families, loving means thinking and feeling just alike. Since this is impossible, family members have a great fear of honest, straightforward encounter, and develop the belief that leveling with family members is tantamount to death—of oneself or the partner. This fear of death is often symbolic, but in many cases it is accompanied by ominous thoughts of possible violence or magical fears of destruction resulting from "wrong" thinking or statements that disobey family rules.

It is essential to recognize that feelings come in pairs, and that understanding oneself or others depends on appreciating human ambivalence. The question, "Does he *really* love me?" often indicates a family belief that people have one basic feeling—love or hate—a belief which inevitably leads to distancing and blandness or to the despairing conclusion that the other is unloving because of previous expressions of anger. The destructive tendency of troubled couples to rehash the past can be traced to this misapprehension. "You really said you hated me." "No I didn't—I said sometimes I almost hated you." "That's the same thing." "*No it isn't.*" And the escalation continues. This fruitless, frustrating, and bleak prosecuting attorney approach can only be interrupted by focusing on current interactions and accepting that one can really be loving and hating at different times—and sometimes at the same time. Only with this shared understanding is it safe to express unguarded feelings.

Anger ≠ Love

Where loyalty is understood as being a clone, much of a therapist's work consists of providing a safe place where people can express "disloyal," "unloving," and even hateful feelings and then reinterpreting them as simply human, to be respected and used.

Once it is explicit, the old rule, "Loving means thinking and feeling just alike," can be replaced with, "You have to be separate to be close." The new rule allows, even requires, each person to express his or her own experience and to listen for the other's useful differences and perceptions.

A peculiar kind of boundary problem occurs when one or both partners have escaped from a "swallowing" kind of family—that is, one whose amorphous boundaries threaten the necessary integration of a self. With such a history individuals are wary of sharing; they remain overtly polite and obstinately bland. The boundary of the self is surrounded by a moat, guarded jealously and replete with usually unconscious memories of past invasions and frightening confusion. The therapist's work is required to encourage feeling statements, to make the treatment environment safe, and to reward tentative expressions. A person must experience success in order to increase these halting efforts at honesty. Modeling by the therapist is of vital importance. After rapport with a couple has been established, the therapist can be blunt and openly expressive even of angry feelings; indeed, a compulsive sweetness on the part of the therapist can reinforce the patient's fear that intimacy is impossible and that the best one can expect is a polite non-aggression pact.

By far the most painful aspect of dealing with couples from severely dysfunctional families is their *despair*. Members believe and expect that everything comes to naught, people are deprived and depriving, and family life is a game with no winners, only losers. This despair is certainly more intense than that found in less disturbed couples. The primary treatment goal is to provide experiences of coherence, establishing that neither partner is destroyed by clarity or by the expression of mixed feelings. Firmly held beliefs in the danger of self-exposure are gradually replaced. Then, the next goal is to help partners identify family rules and provide experiences in choosing whether to change their rules.

Case Example. A profoundly depressed woman, previously in individual psychotherapy for many years, and her husband were referred after two earlier attempts at marital treatment had been abruptly terminated. In our second session, she began to attack.

Mrs. S.: "I can't trust you! You flake out on me when I need you! When I got pregnant and you made me have the abortion, no matter what I said, I learned you can't take care of me."

Mr. S.: "How can I make you believe me? I love you and want only to make you happy."

The husband had always managed to present himself as the good guy.

In the succeeding session, her depression was reframed as a painful but necessary means of testing him, useful for both. By providing him with a way to prove his love, she showed her caring for him. In addition, her tendency to shout and spew out hostility was taken quite seriously—a magical tub was provided for the gallons and gallons of "bile."

Following this session the husband's impotence was revealed by the wife to the therapist. Her assumption of center stage to shout about his untrustworthiness was reframed as further protection of her husband: She was loyally and lovingly taking care of him once again, insuring that he did not have to talk about things that might be frightening or embarrassing. Thus, ambivalence about each other, about her depression, about his symbolic and actual impotence, and about her shouting were brought out in order to begin coherent encounters that acknowledged a mixture of feelings rather than spurious certainty. Yes, she did want to stay married even if she complained a great deal; yes, he did want to have a sexual relationship, even if he had made no move or statement in that direction. We could then entertain some possibility of negotiating.

Trust

In this group of couples, a striking phenomenon regarding paranoid thinking is most evident: Their paranoid thinking (defined as "doctrinaire mistrust") is directly related to the persistence of a childlike trust—the child's absolute trust in a parent, no matter how defective that parent is.

Case Example. Continuing with abovementioned couple, Mrs. S. was stuck in a miserable paranoid state regarding her husband as long as she defined "trustworthy" as not ever letting a loved one down. He had a similar assumption; though he objected to her attacks, he also believed that they were justified because he had indeed let her down. When all the things that had seemed certain and clear in their marriage—her depression and rage, his impotence, his betrayal, his kindness—were given alternative meanings, there was an implied message about the relativity of trust.

"Help other people not hurt you" is a recommendation I frequently offer for getting along with others. The awareness of ambivalence is, in its own way, an awareness of relative trust. The therapist, by presenting himself or herself as limited, possessed of only another perception, not *the* perception, demonstrates the concept that no one is trustworthy as a child would have it; most people are relatively trustworthy if you help them to be so.

Psychosis in Marriage

I never treat a manic patient without including some family members, and my preferred family member, if available, is the spouse. Such spouses have similar behavior patterns;

they are involved in intense efforts at control and have some significant areas of shared magical thinking.

The patient recovering from a severe manic episode is usually at risk of deterioration without lithium, and I usually learn that the spouse is responsible for the medicine. Simple but profound content issues like these—who decides when and how and whether medication is taken—provide opportunities to clarify boundaries (the blurring often having been accentuated by conventional medical treatment). I have an axiom, communicated to patients, that one assumes only those responsibilities that are required by one's existence.

My experience in treating schizophrenic patients has usually involved seeing the schizophrenic within a whole family context rather than as one member of a couple (9, 11); however, clinical research data indicate strongly that involving any family members in the treatment of schizophrenics is superior to no family work at all (23, 29). My clinical experience suggests that the general approach of this book— the focus on relationships, communication, boundaries, and choice—is effective and relatively safe with couples in which one partner has been schizophrenic. This approach is less likely than treatment focused on intrapsychic material (motives, intent, unconscious purposes) to produce emotional stress leading to decompensation.

With reference to therapeutic safety, the uselessness and probable harm of focusing on motives can be emphasized. Severely dysfunctional families are already preoccupied with motives: "Did you intend to. . . ?" can be more important in such families than "What did you do?" I recommend assuming that people want to succeed, want to belong to a family or family-like arrangement, and are morally neutral. They would rather have fun than be miserable, and will respond to positive rewards by increasing whatever is rewarded. These assumptions eliminate most of what is damaging in the severely dysfunctional family rules. The person who is prone toward schizophrenia has doubts about trust: "Does he really love me?" "Is he telling all the truth?" "Why is she so friendly?" Such rumination by patient or therapist can be endless and counterproductive. That healthier couples better tolerate this kind of treatment focus does not prove its effectiveness.

Triangles

Triangles, a problem for every couple in trouble, are particularly tenacious, knotty, and persistent in severely dysfunctional families. Most common are triangles involving the couple and parents or children. They result from the extreme difficulty these malfunctioning families have in accepting losses due to growth and development, aging and death; partners in these marriages, even of 30 years' duration, often feel closer to "blood kin" than to their spouses.

My strategy consists of bringing out the ambivalence, getting everybody but the therapist confused rather than absolutely certain, finding that the partners are on the same side, and then sorting out the triangles with a now strengthened couple bond.

Case Example. Mr. and Ms. S., mentioned earlier, had a 24-year-old son still living at home. Steve was Mrs. S.'s son from a previous marriage; the S.'s married when Steve was three. Mrs. S. Had never been able to believe that Mr. S. cared about this boy, and she felt called upon to protect *her* son from criticism and economic want. For his part, Mr. S. alternated between hostile criticism of Steve and attempts to prove his love for the boy.

We established that they both wanted good things for Steve, that sometimes it is important to be generous, and that sometimes limit-setting and strictness are useful. Further pushing the ambivalence, it was suggested that leaving home is important for growing up, yet everyone needs to feel loved by parents. Mrs. S.'s caring was important, as was Mr. S.'s belief that Steve needed to be on his own. Perhaps Steve might be helping to keep the marital partners at each other's throats, even though he individually desired to grow up, leave home, and have them at peace with each other.

Slowly, tentatively, the couple began to make some decisions together regarding Steve. With reference to Steve's lonely existence, a slogan was offered: "Everybody has to learn to say goodbye in order to learn to say hello." The operational definition of love was broadened from caring and supporting to having expectations of Steve's ability to function outside the family.

COUPLES FROM BORDERLINE FAMILIES

Couples from borderline families make up about 40 percent of my private practice; they are often the most difficult group to treat, and most who come to my office have had several treatment experiences of one sort or another. They can be identified by their extreme concern with control, and yet their incoherence, confusion and frank lunacy are equally certain to seep through the control efforts. Control methods are frequently so extreme as to be bizarre; for example, there can be terrible scenes with one spouse running from room to room to avoid conversation and locking himself or herself in the bathroom, whereupon the partner tears the door down.

As with the most dysfunctional group, far more centripetal than centrifugal borderline families are represented in intensive treatment, since the centrifugal borderline families will not stay in voluntary treatment after a crisis settles down. The centrifugal group will be seen much more often in public and sliding-scale clinics, and even then the treatment unit is rarely the couple.

Treatment always involves a struggle for control. Family members, immersed in their own efforts to control or to avoid control, also wish/fear that the therapist will effectively tyrannize the family. The family system reaches to enmesh the therapist in its continuing, futile struggles. One might characterize couples treatment in this group as avoiding traps. With these couples, I am most likely to be indirect, using a great number of seemingly off-the-wall stories, prescriptions of present dynamics, and apparent encouragement of symptoms. I rarely feel close to these couples or very trusting of them (in contrast to some severely dysfunctional and most midrange couples) until after several months of work.

I use stories with every couple, but more frequently with this group. With stories, I can derail linear control efforts and attain at least a bit of confusion, if not enlightenment. For example, these are a few of the stories I have used with success.

Non-linear behavior. The drunk is looking everywhere in his office—under chairs, under the desk, under the couch. A friend drops by, asks him what he's looking for. He answers, "I've lost my billfold." The friend says, "Have you tried your back pocket?" Our drunk answers, "No, because if I look there and it isn't there, I'll kill myself."

Irrational rationality. The weaving figure is on his hands and knees, at midnight, searching for something under a streetlight. A cop comes by and asks what he's looking for. "I'm looking for my billfold." The cop starts looking too, and asks, "Where did you lose it?" "Oh, in the alley down the street." "What? Then why look here?" "Because the light is better here!"

Include-me-out games. Groucho applied for membership in a posh country club. After not hearing anything from them for quite a while, he wrote, "I withdraw my application from your club. I refuse to associate with anyone who would accept the likes of me."

The Navajo sing. Navajos have an interesting custom. When faced with great trouble or threat, they use words, not for communication with each other, but for impact on the gods. The same words are repeated over and over, in the hope that the gods will be moved.

Homespun paradox. The fox finally caught Bre'r Rabbit and contemplated what terrible thing he would do to him, now that he was helpless. "Do anything you want, Bre'r Fox, but just please don't throw me in the briar patch." The fox figured if that was what Bre'r Rabbit didn't want, then that was what he'd get, so he pitched him in the briars. Bre'r Rabbit bounded off, shouting, "Thanks Bre'r Fox; I was born and raised in the briar patch."

The power of suggestion. A man buys cheap carpets and sells them for a thousand dollars each as magic carpets, guaranteed to fly. He gives a money-back guarantee that the carpets will do what they are promised to do. Yet he has never had to pay back any of the money that he has received for these carpets because he tells the buyer, "There's just one thing, one thing, that you have to remember when you are using this magic carpet, and that is, if you think of a rhinoceros when you are sitting on the carpet it will not move. So under no circumstances may you in any fashion think of a rhinoceros or the word rhinoceros while you are planning to take off."

Control effort. The French politician looked out over his balcony and saw a huge mob surging toward the Chamber of Deputies. He quickly called an aide, saying, "I must follow them, for I am their leader."

More control by not controlling. When my son was three and a half (he is now an ancient who hates this story), I was a do-it-yourselfer, and had a workbench and tool cabinet in my garage. Underneath, I had built him a miniature work bench and cabinet. We were working away one Saturday morning, and I, having lost my hammer temporarily, reached down and grabbed his. He drew himself up to his full 2 and ¾ feet and said, benevolently, "I will *let* you use my hammer."

Zany stories, funny stories, stories that speak of nonlinear thinking, behavior, and results can break up simplistic cause-and-effect control efforts. Many times the stories are of previous families and their ingenious efforts to get satisfaction by sterile control.

The so-called "paradoxical interventions" (32) are most appropriate with this group. I refer to them as "so-called" because there is good reason to believe that paradoxical interventions work only when they are not paradoxical. Success with strategic interventions (such as telling a couple to go slow in change; recommending the continuation of a symptom; prescribing present, apparently maladaptive, couple or family patterns; inviting a spouse to stage-manage a bitterly resented marital pattern) may result from their making sense and being, in a very real sense, logical! Their use illustrates that the therapist understands the couple.

A problem with paradoxical intervention is the impossibility for an observer to determine with certainty when a paradoxical intervention has been made. To do so would require knowing things that are not observable, such as:

What is the intent of the therapist?

What is the meaning of the statement to the couple or family members?

To use paradox effectively, I believe it is necessary to understand that symptoms are *both* an expression of individual and marital or family conflict *and* an effort to solve that conflict. Described in this way, symptoms have a great deal in common with successful adaptation. The difference is that symptomatic behavior works badly and is characterized by stereotyped interaction and psychic pain rather than pleasure and satisfaction. Realizing this allows the therapist, like the French politician, to remain in control of forces that could trample an unwise would-be leader.

Additionally, the effective use of paradox requires recognition of ambivalence. Patients must be aware of mixed feelings and experience the opportunity of choice before the resolution of these mixed feelings can occur. Finally, the inextricable relationship of individual ambivalence to family conflict must be acknowledged. Each is related to the other, neither can occur without the other, and neither is resolved without the other.

Case Example. Mark, a 46-year-old executive, quarreled constantly with Audrey, his wife of 24 years, who had disseminated lupus, a potentially lethal collagen disease which produces dysfunction and some pain. After being in treatment with a variety of individual therapists for many years, they decided to try marital therapy. It went poorly, in that their pattern of bitter attacks on each other did not diminish. The therapist told them that perhaps they should continue to fight regularly, since this activity was most important in 1) preventing Mark's realization that Audrey was weak, ill, and could die (as long as they fought, he could see her as powerful and even omnipotent); and 2) avoiding Audrey's experience of Mark as loving her and looking out for her. Defining herself as unloved, Audrey was compelled to be fiercely independent and believed this kept her alive.

The results of the paradoxical prescription were, in the short term, striking. Their battles subsided and they experienced a new gentleness and mutual expressions of caring. However, there were side effects: Both partners slipped into depressed states that were painful to experience or observe. Mark, Audrey, and the therapist seemed relieved when the quarrels resumed.

This vignette illustrates many of the points of the preceding discussion. The long-term failure of the paradoxical intervention in keeping the couple free of the quarrels, which they both wanted to end, was, I believe, related to Audrey's illness. The specter of death and loss can make attractive the kind of ritualized, stereotyped behavior that expresses unresolved ambivalence and keeps people suspended, neither leaving nor getting too close. In other instances, of course, the symptoms are no longer needed when adaptive behavior replaces the symptomatic.

COUPLES FROM MIDRANGE FAMILIES

Couples from this group also make up about 40 percent of my patient load. They are usually the easiest and most gratifying people to treat, comparable to the mythic "well-motivated, verbal, intelligent neurotics" of individual psychotherapy. Just as some airplanes and computers are described as "forgiving," these couples will stay with a therapist and improve even though he or she makes many technical errors. This is due to their family experiences; their parents, though control oriented, were able to resolve ambivalence well enough to prevent these parents from being frightening and incoherent to small children. In other words, the individuals in these marriages expect an authority figure to make sense and will make allowances for human frailty.

I will describe midrange mixed and midrange centripetal couple treatment together; as stated earlier, the midrange centrifugal couple or family seldom stays in treatment. Individuals in these pairings are frustrated because someone has let them down. A child may be defined as the villain, and perhaps prior work has moved the treatment focus to the couple. Often, however, each person feels that the other has been disappointing, and they have oscillated between intimidation and playing to the referee. Experience of and some hope for intimacy are present. In these couples despair is significantly less than in the other treatment groups, and the period of demoralization is relatively short-lived.

Control is what these people want, and control is what they get—with a twist. Since they hunger for intimacy as well as control, I state the following within the first few sessions:

1) Control is good; control everything that you can.
2) People do not come to me because they are controlling; they come because their present methods are unsuccessful.
3) There is a tragedy in the fact that many people wish for intimacy with spouses, parents or children, yet use intimidation, a method which is doomed to fail.
4) "The gift without the giver is bare." One longs for children to *want* to take out the trash rather than sullenly complying, spouses who *want* to have more or less sex, rather than halfheartedly going along, partners who prepare special meals or who come home on time because they *desire* to.
5) Therefore, control aimed at intimacy in any human transaction requires attention to the choices of the parties involved.
6) Negotiations can then be completed where everybody wins.

This is the framework for much of my work with mid-range families.

There are, of course many other considerations with couples from this group. For example, the issue of truth is always important. These couples are more apt to be influenced by society's fads, since they are the most socialized of the treatment groups. When learning how to fight is "in," expressed honest anger is viewed as virtuous; while this tends toward middle-class couples aping lower-class couples, it usually does little to increase negotiating skills. I have seen couples virtuously and futilely venting rage and being hurtful in an effort to heal their marriage. More time and effort are required to get at deeper honesty. In any powerful and passionate circumstance, individuals experience many different feelings, and these people have to make some choices as to which of their many feelings are expressed.

For example, Dick and Jane are arguing over money. Their arrangement is that he brings home the paycheck and she pays the bills and keeps the records. He feels he never has any money of his own; she feels she is always second-guessed as to her spending. He tries to get her to be reasonable, that is, spend less; she tries to get him to be reasonable; that is, respect inflation and her skills in keeping the family solvent.

There is anger here, of course. There is also hurt: Why don't you see that I am a good person trying to do the best I can? And there is guilt: Dick believes he could make more money if he applied himself; Jane was always criticized by her father for having no head for figures. In addition there is fear: We argue so much, should we have married? Will our marriage survive?

Any and all of these feelings are honest. A good therapist will help people express the feelings that go best with the needs and goals of the people involved. In troubled mid-range centripetal marriages, there are additional problems produced by the family rules that 1) loving feelings should be expressed, 2) angry feelings are bad, 3) one should be loyal to one's loved ones and to one's commitments.

With such rules, anger must be accompanied by justification; it can only be righteous indignation or it is out of bounds. So frustration, which produces anger, then produces moralizing and intimidation. Not only are there many feelings in a frustrating situation, but fixed family rules produce attitudes of righteous attack and virtuous defense.

It is with such couples that an appeal to self-interest and practicality is most effective. The therapist can bless selfishness or self-interest, reframing it as being responsible for oneself. She or he can have the "linebacker's stance" of continually asking, "What do you want?" "How are you trying to get it?" This is the touchstone of a relationship mode that encourages individual differentiation and choice-making.

Dreams

Only with midrange couples will I respond positively to efforts at telling dreams. More disturbed families have such a vivid waking behavior illustrating needed changes that it is a poor use of time to encourage dream material. In midrange couples, however, dreams can be quite useful in intensifying feelings and bringing the participants' attention to neglected areas, as well as increasing a sense of lightness and imaginative play in family interaction.

I firmly believe that "interpretation" of dreams merely represents a way of developing and maintaining an overt power edge; that is, a therapist is imposing a world view on a willing subject. Rather than interpret dreams, with the attendant development of a power hierarchy, I suggest that dreams are a continuation of our life experience into sleep; consequently, the material can be useful even though the language is different. It is a language of metaphor, images, analogies and patterns. Anyone can play with a dream and one person's thoughts on the matter are as good as another's. (Children are particularly able to respond to dreams without feeling the need to have a "correct" answer to their meaning.) Spouses' discussions of dreams can reduce power differences and encourage intimacy.

The Family Referee

People always experience events differently; conflicted family members never understand this and spend their lives with unresolved ambivalence and struggle. The family ref-

222   *Successful Marriage*

eree, rather than arbitrary human authority, controls the midrange family: "It is not what *I* say but what everyone (and no specific one) says is right and proper that should be followed."

These "shoulds," placed on individuals by family systems and then clutched desperately by the same tyrannized people, are the source of much emotional disturbance. They can be contrasted usefully with "want-to's" and "have-to's." "Want-to's" are self-defined desires with both power and vulnerability; "want-to's" can be thwarted, delayed, attacked and ridiculed, with resulting but not persistent emotional distress. "Have-to's," similarly, do not have the guilt-inducing capacity of "shoulds." For instance, "I have to pay my bills in order to keep up my credit rating," or, "I have to feed my children so they do not starve." "Have-to's" are not moral but technical. Between "want-to's" and "have-to's" we cover the waterfront of adult functioning. Self-definition thrives on "I want," is limited by "I have to," and is threatened and damaged by "I should."

The couples therapist is negotiating constantly, using these concepts and working to reduce the "shoulds." A powerful weapon is the completion of sentences! "I should have sex with my wife/husband—if I enjoy it (want to), or if I wish to keep him/her (have to)." "I should spend the time with the children—if I want them to know and like me (want to), or if they will not feel emotionally deprived (have to)." Every "should" left undefined is a projection and a source of guilt or resentment; it can be eliminated or converted to a useful ego or self orientation.

Many couples come to treatment with a shared razor's edge. On one side is resentment and on the other, guilt—the natural result of growing up in a midrange family complete with an inhuman referee. Each person attempts to solve relationship problems by following and prescribing the referee's rules, and no solution is free from psychic pain.

"If I get my way, I feel guilty, but if you get your way, I feel resentful." This is an expression of the underlying belief that one person's advantage comes from another's pain or frustration, and vice versa. A significant goal with these midrange couples is to change this assumption to another: "My satisfaction increases the chances that you are pleasured, and your enjoyment will increase my own." It is easy for couples to experience this with me—no one has difficulty perceiving that I am delighted when spouses leave a session feeling good and believing they received a lot. So their experience with a relative stranger can be moved into another arena—that of experience with the lover/spouse.

These couples are capable of learning the skills necessary for intimacy. Challenging the "shoulds," providing experience in "I win, you win," rewarding honest expressed need, blessing ambivalence and encouraging its resolution with the resultant choice, can help individuals become more satisfied with marriage—usually with the spouse they have.

There is one other concept/technique particularly applicable to midrange couples. This is "helping others not hurt you." As "shoulds" give way to needs, as intimidation gives way to a variety of techniques for achieving intimacy and gratification, they learn to see the partner as grown-up yet vulnerable and, in some ways, ignorant. Relative, not absolute, trust is necessary for building a relationship, and this means that no person—not parent, lover, spouse, or therapist—can be trusted with the responsibility for another. We all have blind spots and need to be helped in order not to hurt.

I find many opportunities to illustrate this in my own involvement with the pair. I sometimes forget and need to be reminded. Sometimes I don't attend well, and patients must press hard if they feel I haven't heard. Both partners may have to work on me before I get an important point. I don't create these opportunities by playing dumb; they will occur in spite of my best efforts! As couples realize this and "go the second mile" in helping me to help them, there is valuable fallout in their relationship.

With this group of couples, I use a few handouts. Here is one that has produced comments, laughter and sometimes change.

Lessons From a Dancing Chicken

Family members are always trying to get somebody else to do something—husbands should be more affectionate, wives should ask for more (or less) sex, children should start doing something or stop it. If the family members are particularly inept in implementing such desires, they may seek out a family therapist.

Like most therapists, I have a variety of strategies to help a family regulate itself better, but I do rely a good bit on teaching and learning. For that reason I frequently tell a story about an Arkansas boy who went north, ran into a fellow named Skinner who taught him how to do such things as make a chicken dance. Or play baseball, or ride a fire engine. Such a wondrous knowledge should be shared, so he went back to Arkansas and opened up an establishment called the I.Q. Zoo, a cornucopia of fabulous animal feats.

Now if an ordinary person can make a chicken dance, surely you can get your husband (wife, son, daughter, parent) to_____ (fill in the blank). It's a matter of knowing how.

First off, you must believe the chicken isn't evil, isn't making every attempt to thwart your hopes and dreams. It's hard to train a chicken if you think it has it in for you.

Second, you reward the chicken with something the chicken likes, not with what you think he ought to like or with whatever's handy. (For humans probably the most powerful reward is a moment of shared delight.)

Third, you reward *approximations* of the behavior desired. If you wait until the chicken spins all the way around before rewarding, you will have a long time between opportunities to be effective. A turn of the head to the left, a foot moving in that dirrection will merit a quick reward.

Fourth, you ignore behavior that is not what you want—we would call it undancing behavior. The combination of alert rewards and careful neglect of the unwanted is a powerful tool in producing a dancing chicken.

Fifth, punishment is not necessary in creating dancing chickens, but it can discourage some other behaviors and therefore might have some usefulness. However, its power of discouraging is only brought out in the presence of a background of steady and expected rewards for desired behavior that override the punishment in frequency and in intensity. A starved chicken just doesn't dance or do much of anything else very well. Without the contrasting reward, punishment becomes a reward and encourages that which it is supposed to diminish or prohibit.

Once told, the tale is a kind of halltree on which to hand various bits of family interaction. "He never does_____." Okay, what would be the motivation for such obstinacy? What would be a prized and pleasing reward for a bit of_____that he never does? Has the family overlooked most of the powerful reinforcers, such as the shared satisfactions of working together, laughing together over a bit of silliness, enjoying the other's mere presence?

One can ask the chicken to become a collaborator, discussing what rewards would be effective. In this way, negotiating skills evolve.

One more element is needed. A family rule must be imposed: "The responsibility for change and the *desire* for change, because of pain, hurt, dream or wish, must be kept within the same person." This allows the context to be clear as to who is chicken and who is trainer at a given time. This rule plus the principle of the dancing chicken can help many families break frustrating patterns and build satisfying ones.

SEXUAL ISSUES

It is unusual for troubled partners to be content regarding their sexual life. This is frequently not the presenting complaint, however; the initial despair, problems and pain are much more likely to be the shared focus than enjoyment or even a wish for enjoyment. I have found it useful to think and speak of sexual difficulties as problems of *interest in* or *enthusiasm during* sexual activity. These two categories cover "secondary impotence" (primary impotence in couples therapy is a rarity) frigidity, premature and delayed ejaculation, and problems with sexual desire (33). The overly precise labeling of sexual dysfunction in discrete entities tends to isolate them from individuals and relationships, as if they existed in a vacuum rather than in an interpersonal context. With this orientation, I find that few people I treat have sexual dysfunction that is unrelated to the presenting marital problems. Premature ejaculations melts into "You come before I'm ready"; retarded ejaculation becomes "You come long after I am tired." Both events are viewed as interpersonal and relative—to be defined by the couple rather than by the doctor or therapist. I find it peculiar, constructive, and sometimes humorous that we in the healing business often recreate pathological interaction with families by accepting the role of powerful definer and then struggle with the other person's difficulties, while the other person remains ungratified and takes satisfaction only in defeating our authority.

Even though the initial evaluation includes a request to talk about sexual issues, serious work in this area may be delayed for weeks or months. I have found it important to follow a couple's lead and not to insist that sexual problems be addressed early in treatment. Many people are sensitive to real or imagined sexual defects; when their self-esteem is low, the therapist's approaching these in an aggressive manner can demoralize them further. I frequently remind myself that it is the couple's agenda, not mine, that is to be attended in order to have an experience in shared power. I have technical expertise; they have need and potential choice. Sexual difficulties usually mirror the relationship problems; that is, like many other symptoms, they can be viewed as metaphors for the relationship.

Case Example. Mr. and Mrs. V. are a remarried couple. Mr. V. complained of Mrs. V.'s *compliance*—she never refused his sexual entreaties, but her acquiescense was so docile, so unresponsive, as to move him to mayhem. Here is/is not a sexual difficulty. Mr. and Mrs. V. could and did have intercourse and they did have a complaint about their sexual relationship; however the problem most urgently in need of recognition was their graphic enactment of a slave/master(or mistress) relationship. He was in control as he demanded sex and she complied; she was in control as she withheld enthusiasm and he went berserk. One part of Mr. V. had been defining his wife as his mother, who was in his eyes both pitiful and controlling; another part was desperately trying to be a responsible adult. Mrs. V. was struggling with her family of origin's message that women who enjoy sex are whores. She used her husband as a control mechanism, appreciating and resenting him at the same time.

Biological problems relative to sexual difficulties, for example, diabetes, neurological illnesses, and medication-induced performance problems, must be considered. It is horrifying to encounter spouses who have been dealt with by a simplistic assumption that the interaction is responsible for the impotence of the husband, only to discover, after a proper physical examination, that the husband's diabetic condition is the primary source of his problems. The therapist, whatever his discipline, must think many levels of systems when defining problems and their cure. Sexual problems illustrate perhaps the most dramatic need for such a multilevel approach.

Sexual problems of frequency and enthusiasm that are clearly related to interpersonal, rather than organic and biological, factors can be dealt with first by direct means. Desensitization methods such as those used by Kaplan (33) can clear up many problems of secondary impotence. The couple is forbidden intercourse and instructed to pleasure each other without genital stimulation; following success with this exercise, they are instructed to include genital stimulation. The frequency and the lengths of these exercises are negotiated with the couple. As performance anxiety lessens and sexual play resurfaces, sexual capability will usually return. Often, however, the couple's failure to carry out the agreed-on tasks becomes a focus of work for a time as the advantages of a nonsexual relationship are explored.

Performance anxiety for women is on the increase; with increasing media attention, orgasm during intercourse and especially simultaneous orgasm are thought to be a requirement for normal sexual functioning. Many women are orgasmic only with greater stimulation than that which occurs in intercourse. I reassure couples that only 47 percent of pairings have shared orgasm during intercourse. (This is an honest quote, which could as easily be 40 percent or 55 percent due to inexact polling methodology.) I like to suggest that, since less than half of the known world is able to do what the couple is trying to accomplish, if they succeed, they can consider themselves sexually elite; if they continue having orgasms by manual or oral means, they are normal. In this way, the emphasis is on personal enjoyment rather than sexual Olympics.

DIVORCE

In looking over the last two hundred couples that I have seen, several patterns regarding divorce become apparent. About three-quarters of the couples from severely dysfunctional families divorce within three years after initiating treatment; only one-quarter of the couples from borderline and midrange families divorced in a three-year follow-up period. I was surprised that severely dysfunctional couples had such a high rate. Since most were from centripetal families, the inability to hold the lid on conflict, as evidenced by seeking marital treatment, apparently reflects more instability of marital ties than that evidenced when marital treatment is sought by the other groups. The second surprise was the tenacity of the borderline group in staying together; they are as likely to do so as the midrange couples. I would have expected a parallel relationship between degree of dysfunction and frequency of divorce.

I always make some statement of my views on divorce early in couples treatment. I emphasize that determining individual choice is important to me, that it has been my experience that people are ambivalent about staying together or divorcing and that the choice to do either is usually a joint decision. This offers me an opportunity to raise a systems issue: Usually one person will be the voice of the ambivalence, because the system requires only one person's expression of it to make the uncertainty real for both. When one partner resolves mixed feelings by opting for marriage, frequently the other partner, previously having shown every sign of wanting to continue in harness, waffles and becomes the new carrier of uncertainty.

The goals of treatment, then, do not include maintaining the marriage unless that is the stated desire of both partners. I do offer that more of the treated couples remain together than decide to part; this emphasizes choice but invites the partners' efforts to see if they can live together enjoyably. Recognizing that divorce does occur in troubled marriages and is accompanied by a sense of personal failure, this approach seems to lessen the pain of marital dissolution.

The Bull-speak Quotient

In my couples sample, divorce is concentrated in two periods—early in treatment and after a rather long time of generally turbulent treatment. The early group has sought treatment as a last gasp effort, and I counsel these people as follows:

There is a concept that is most important for every person thinking of divorce. This is the bull-speak quotient (B.S.Q.), defined as the degree that one's talking and feeling and acting are congruent, or how much one's behavior tracks with verbal communication. Poor tracking equals high B.S.Q.; good tracking, low B.S.Q. Troubled couples have been struggling, playing to the referee, and they get convoluted to the point that each individual has a high B.S.Q. My job as therapist is to help both partners to lower this quotient as determined by the persons involved. This means we will work the same way to get a good marriage as to get a good divorce.

If a spouse believes she or he has done a good job of becoming congruent, a dramatic change for the better will usually be shown by the partner. If this does not occur, then the person will at least know why she or he is divorcing and have a reasonably sound belief that a new relationship can be developed with greater skills and more honesty. A low B.S.Q. is to be treasured; it helps relative trust to blossom.

I believe a good therapist must maintain a low B.S.Q. as well. When one "puts a twist on the ball"—becomes cute or manipulative—one never knows whether the responses are related to the other's functioning or to one's own. In the midst of frustrating times during treatment, I find it most reassuring to be able to review the case and find that I have been honest as well as professional. I believe that intensive psychotherapy is one of a few ways to make a living that encourages maintaining a low B.S.Q.

Divorce Late in Treatment or Following

Late divorces represent only a small percent of my couples sample. This is fortunate; they are painful to me as well as to the partners. We three have invested a great deal of energy in this enterprise, and divorce has an impact, even though we have agreed to define success as the resolution of ambivalence rather than as their going hand in hand toward the sunset. The reasons for late divorces differ.

Case Example. Mr. and Mrs. I. were, to all available evidence, mismatched. He was a violently prejudiced redneck; she was active in the Urban League and just about every other cause. He liked to go to their farm in an old pickup; she liked the symphony and her liberal church. Nevertheless, when they were seen with their teenagers, the whole family expressed joy and liveliness that was dramatically missing when the two were by themselves.

The I.'s were in treatment to develop some ability to talk, to respect each other, and to have some enjoyable sex. This they accomplished. However, as soon as the three oldest left home, the parents split; the glue that had held them together was the vitality of their offspring.

Case Example. Mr. and Mrs. Q. were remarried with "his and hers" children. They were seen as a family and later as a couple dealing with relationship issues in a frequently explosive fashion. They settled down, had a "conversion" to marital bliss and left treatment after six months. About six months later, Mrs. Q. called just to let me know that they had separated and were divorcing, and she felt much better. In the 10 years since I worked with this couple, I believe I have learned much more about stepfamilies. I do not know, however, whether my relative lack of attention to the special factors involved influenced this divorce following a seemingly good treatment result.

Case Example. Mr. and Mrs. U. had worked hard in marital therapy. She had gone from cartoon hysteric to an attractive, thinking woman who was assertive but not assaultive. He had moved from a cartoon wimpish rich man's son to a young man with confidence and a personal viewpoint. But they did not develop a sense of loving and desire for each other for which they both longed. They agreed to divorce, and a number of sessions were devoted to arranging for their two children, for housing and for financial security. Marital therapy had become divorce therapy (34). Mr.

and Mrs. U. remained friends and both have since remarried. The therapist has seen the two new couples and both remarriages have gone well.

The U.'s are a textbook example of how marital therapy leading to divorce could and should go. Choice-making was strengthened, individual self-esteem and confidence increased, and both people have done well and have been content after divorce. The therapist continued to be perceived as a friend to both.

TERMINATION, LOSS, AND TRANSCENDENT VALUES

It may seem odd that I include loss and termination in the same section, but they seem to me related. With every individual, couple, or family in whom I have invested part of my life, and who go their way, I have a sense of loss. My own children have left home and established careers. I still grieve at times for the old days, when they were opening up to the world and I could provide them with opportunities and information. We still have enjoyable times together, but now we are clearly equals, and I am more apt to receive information about the world than to offer it. There has been a loss, along with development of a new and appreciated relationship that was the goal of parenting. The mixed feelings are the same with patients and, in this context, with couples. I rejoice at their increasing skills and satisfactions and feel, with every step toward responsible autonomy, the poignancy of inevitable termination.

"You have to learn to say goodbye before you can learn to say hello." This is true of patient and therapists. I have experienced the loss of a thousand patients; the fact that these losses have produced people who are defined in the world as acceptable and successful makes the task worthwhile but doesn't do away with some pain. Growth and development produce a sense of loss equal to, though easier to accept, than death.

Living successfully requires the capacity to handle losses

and to renew oneself by developing new caring relationships. This is true with marriages as well as with divorces. The partners who successfully traverse the white waters of the life cycle have related to each other as several spouses; they begin, perhaps, as the naive young bride and the scared young man, then the ambitious executive and the eager-to-help corporation wife, followed by the corporation dropout and newly assertive woman, and finally two aging individuals who struggle to make sense of a changing world. Changes in individuals must be mirrored by changes in the marital structure or the fragile craft will be destroyed on the ever-threatening rocks.

Loss of parents and of children is an expected part of the life cycle; loss of the spouse is equally likely, but not so well publicized or understood. In every instance, there is the possibility of either focusing on the loss and becoming stuck, despairing and hopeless, or looking at the opportunities for change and reaching for the unknown.

Clinically, I have found it most useful to help individuals get in touch with both sides of their strong mixed feelings toward the lost person. In this way, mourning can be completed.

I often think of altering the child's game of musical chairs, a bitter metaphor for life's changes, to have it more accurately represent life's possibilities. In musical chairs, you may remember, the children tramp around a circle of chairs, one of which is removed with each stanza of music. The music stops, there is a frantic rush for seats, and one person is eliminated. Finally, the one person left is designated winner—but there is no one else for the winner to play with. This is how many couples perceive loss; they naturally clutch convulsively at what they have. Instead, the game might be played with several circles of chairs; when a chair is removed from one circle, it becomes a part of a new one; losses and beginnings would be balanced, and no one would be forced to be alone, reflecting the possibilities of loss and rebirth found in real life.

But then, children's games are often expressive of frightening or miserable possibilities of life (witness ring-around-the-rosy originating with the European Black Death of the Dark Ages); perhaps they are aimed at symbolic mastery.

This section is entitled "Termination, Loss, and Transcendent Values." We have dealt with the termination and loss, but where do the transcendent values come in and what are they?

A therapist may define the professional task as helping individuals become unstuck in their relationships and move toward growth. But growth toward what ends? Supporting what values? These are vital questions that an honest therapist does not answer for patients. As more energy is available for living, self-defined values assume practical significance. When spouses become less involved with their shared neurotic patterns, they are restless. The energy freed up produces restlessness, which in turn can be misused to create new neurotic patterns or a regression to the old ones; after all, there has to be some reason to get up in the morning! Otherwise, each member of a couple must do some soul-searching as to what is important in his or her world. Having decided, energy can be invested toward progression rather than regression. Whether family member, therapist, or politician, we ignore mankind's need for values at considerable peril.

The transcendent value or values chosen must meet the following criteria:

1) They must be beyond one's own skin and beyond the skins of family members in order to balance the human fears related to growth and development, aging and death.
2) They must allow for the development of community.

Conventional religions, political goals, and environmental preservation are examples of beliefs that invite group participation and sharing. Common beliefs about what is important and the development of a community that represents those beliefs are the essence of the religious in life. To extend the concept of family to the broader world, so that loss can be balanced by discovery and new love, is essential.

3) They must be capable of adding to the quality of human endeavor. Being *for* something, believing an ideal to be a gift to humanity, allows for identification with winning, even though one faces the final loss of death.

It is remarkable to see couples who previously worshiped at the alter of shared neurosis groping for new meaning and finding it in a variety of human enterprises. The more a couple or member reaches beyond the family for sustenance, the more substance is available for the couple. With lovers, the giving is getting, the getting is giving. With a useful transcendent value system, the same is true in relating to the outside world: Expending energy supports a belief and gives to a community; there is also a reciprocal experience of being gratified and fed.

REFERENCES

1. Ables, B. S., & Brandsma, J. M.: *Therapy for Couples*. San Francisco: Jossey-Bass, 1977.
2. Anonymous: Toward the differentiation of a self in one's own family. In J. L. Framo (Ed.), *Family Interaction: A Dialogue between Family Researchers and Family Therapists*. New York: Springer, 1972.
3. Appleton, W. S.: Mistreatment of patients' families by psychiatrists. *American Journal of Psychiatry, 131,* 6:655–657, 1975.
4. Beavers, W. R.: A theoretical basis for family evaluation. In J. M. Lewis, W. R. Beavers, J. T. Gossett, & V. A. Phillips, *No Single Thread: Psychological Health in Family Systems*. New York: Brunner/Mazel, 1976.
5. Beavers, W. R.: *Psychotherapy and Growth: A Family Systems Perspective*. New York: Brunner/Mazel, 1977.
6. Beavers, W. R.: A systems model of family for family therapists. *Journal of Marital and Family Therapy, 7,* 3:299–307, 1981.
7. Beavers, W. R.: Healthy, midrange and severely dysfunctional families. In F. Walsh (Ed.), *Normal Family Processes*. New York: Guilford Press, 1982.
8. Beavers, W. R.: Hierarchical issues in a systems approach to illness and health. *Family Systems Medicine, 1,* 1:44–55, 1983.
9. Beavers, W. R.: Therapy of a family with a schizophrenic member. In S. Coleman (Ed.), *Failures in Family Therapy*. New York: Guilford Press, 1985.
10. Beavers, W. R. and Blumberg, S.: A follow-up study of adolescents treated in an inpatient setting. *Journal of Diseases of the Nervous System, 29,* 606–612, 1968.
11. Beavers, W. R., Blumberg, S., Timken, K. R., & Weiner, M. D.: Communication patterns of mothers of schizophrenics. *Family Process, 4,* 1:95–104, 1965.
12. Beavers, W. R., & Kaslow, F. W.: The anatomy of hope. *Journal of Marital and Family Therapy, 7,* 2:119–126, 1981.
13. Beavers, W. R., & Voeller, M. N.: Family models: Comparing the

Olson circumplex model with the Beavers systems model. *Family Process*, 22, 1:85–98, 1983.

14. Bergin, A. E.: Further comments on psychotherapy research and therapeutic practice. *International Journal of Psychiatry*, 3, 317–323, 1967.
15. Berne, E.: *Games People Play*. New York: Grove Press, 1964.
16. Von Bertalanffy, L.: *General Systems Theory*. New York: George Braziller, 1968.
17. Boss, P. G.: The marital relationship: Boundaries and ambiguities. In H. I. McCubbin & C. R. Figley (Eds.), *Stress and the Family. Vol. 1: Coping With Normative Transitions*. New York: Brunner/Mazel, 1983, pp. 26–40.
18. Boszormenyi-Nagy, I.: Contextual therapy: Therapeutic leverages in mobilizing trust. In R. J. Green & J. L. Framo (Eds.), *Family Therapy: Major Contributions*. New York: International Universities Press, 1981.
19. Davenport, Y. B.: Treatment of the married bipolar patient in conjoint couples psychotherapy groups. In M. R. Lansky (Ed.), *Family Therapy and Major Psychopathology*. New York: Grune & Stratton, 1981.
20. Davenport, Y. B., Ebert, M. H., Adland, M. L., & Goodwin, F. K.: Couples group therapy as an adjunct to lithium maintenance of manic patient. *American Journal of Orthopsychiatry*, 47, 3:495–502, 1977.
21. Davis, F. H.: Patterns in the distortion of scientific method. *Southern Medical Journal*, 53, 1117, 1960.
22. Erikson, E. H.: *Childhood and Society* (2nd ed.). New York: W. W. Norton, 1963.
23. Falloon, I., Boyd, J. L., & McGill, C. W.: *Family Care of Schizophrenics*. New York: Guilford Press, 1984.
24. Fenichel, O.: *The Psychoanalytic Theory of Neurosis*. New York: W. W. Norton, 1945.
25. Ford, F.: personal communication, 1978.
26. Frank, J. *Persuasion and Healing: A Comparative Study of Psychotherapy*. Baltimore: Johns Hopkins University Press, 1961.
27. Freud, S.: Introductory lectures on psychoanalysis (1916–1917). *The Standard Edition*, Vols. XV, XVI. New York: W. W. Norton.
28. Fromm, E.: *Escape from Freedom*. New York: Farrar & Rinehart, 1941.
29. Goldstein, M. S., Rodnick, E. H., Evans, J. R., May, P. R. A., & Steinberg, M. R. Drug and family therapy in the aftercare of acute schizophrenics. *Archives of General Psychiatry*, 35, 1169–1177, 1978.
30. Gurman, A. S. & Kniskern, D. P.: Research on marital and family therapy: Progress, perspective, and prospect. In S. Garfield & A. Bergin (Eds.), *Handbook of Psychotherapy and Behavior Change*. 2nd ed. New York: Wiley, 1978.
31. Haley, J.: *Problem Solving Therapy*. San Francisco: Jossey-Bass, 1977.
32. Hoffman, L.: *Foundations of Family Therapy: A Conceptual Framework for System Change*. New York: Basic Books, 1981.
33. Kaplan, H. S.: *The New Sex Therapy*. New York: Brunner/Mazel, 1974.

34. Kaslow, F. W.: Divorce and divorce therapy. In A. S. Gurman, & D. P. Kniskern (Eds.), *Handbook of Family Therapy*. New York: Brunner/Mazel, 1981.
35. Kohut, H.: *The Restoration of the Self*. New York: International Universities Press, 1977.
36. Lewis, J. M., Beavers, W. R., Gossett, J. T., & Phillips, V. A.: *No Single Thread: Psychological Health in Family Systems*. New York: Brunner/Mazel, 1976.
37. Mahler, M. S.: *The Psychological Birth of the Human Infant: Symbiosis and Individuation*. New York: Basic Books, 1975.
38. Minuchin, S.: *Families and Family Therapy*. Cambridge, MA: Harvard University Press, 1974.
39. Minuchin, S., Rosman, B. C., & Baker, L.: *Psychosomatic Families: Anorexia Nervosa in Context*. Cambridge, MA: Harvard University Press, 1978.
40. Mishler, E., & Waxler, N.: *Interaction in Families*. New York: Wiley, 1968.
41. Olson, D. H., Russell, C. S., & Sprenkle, D. H.: Circumplex model of marital and family systems: VI. Theoretical update. *Family Process*, 22, 1:69–84, 1983.
42. Riskin, J., & Faunce, E. E.: Family interaction scales: III. Discussion of methodology and substantive findings. *Archives of General Psychiatry*, 22, 527–537, 1970.
43. Speck, R., & Attneave, C. L.: *Family Networks*. New York: Pantheon, 1973.
44. Skinner, B. F.: *Beyond Freedom and Dignity*. New York: Knopf, 1971.
45. Stierlin, H.: *Separating Parents and Adolescents*. New York: Quadrangle, 1972.
46. Sullivan, H. S.: *The Interpersonal Theory of Psychiatry*. New York: W. W. Norton, 1953.
47. Walsh, F.: Breaching of family generation boundaries by schizophrenics, disturbed and normals. *International Journal of Family Therapy*, 1, 254–275, 1979.
48. Watzlawick, P., Beavin, J. N., & Jackson, D. D.: *Pragmatics of Human Communication*. New York: W. W. Norton, 1967.
49. Westley, W. S., & Epstein, N. B.: *The Silent Majority*. San Francisco: Jossey-Bass, 1969.

INDEX

behavior (*continued*)
  suicidal, 16, 20, 33–34
  see also specific topics
beliefs, *see* attitudes
Bergin, A. E., 69
Berne, E., 74
Bertalanffy, L. von, 148
bickering, intervention in, 111
Boss, P. G., 152
Boszormenyi-Nagy, I., 191
boundaries:
  clear, 78–79, 81, 122
  defined, 48
  disturbed, 38–40, 48–51, 55, 92–94, 143–44, 171, 177–80
  "swallowing" family and, 38–40, 208
  of therapist, 103
building-a-case pattern, 169
bulimia, 150
bull-speak quotient (B.S.Q.), 229–30

causes, passionate belief in, 75
causes and effects, interchangeability of, 72, 73–74, 101, 131
Centripetal/Centrifugal (CP/CF) dimension, 148–52
certainty, false sense of, 118
chair technique, 62
character structure, successful living and, 117
child abuse, 71
child development, 143
  family dynamics and, 36–38, 54–55
children, 50, 56–57
  adults' intimacy with, 52
  antonomy of, 54, 153
  birth of, 48, 152, 153
  birth order of, 58
  choices made by, 56–57
  divorce and, 154

  dreams of, 221
  emotional problems of, 17–19
  inefficiency of, 155
  of midrange families, 150
  power of, 51
  projecting antisocial feelings onto, 51
  starting school and, 152, 153
choice-making, 30–34, 37, 44, 107, 145, 182–83
  control and, 56–57
  making mistakes and, 54
  masochistic behavior and, 187–88
  respect for, 80–82
  roles and, 59–60, 166
chronic marital conflict, 133–235
  acute marital conflict vs., 141–43
  common problems and solutions in, 157–89
  framework of treatment for, 135–56
  summary of, 155–56, 188–89
clarity, clarifying:
  confusion of then and now, 162
  contextual and contractual, 59–61, 159–66
"cogwheeling," 37
coherence, 151–52, 163, 206, 209
cohesiveness, 148
commitment, 182
  lack of, 20–22, 30, 32–33
communication:
  clarifying of, 162–66
  open, 50–51
  in severely dysfunctional families, 151
community, transcendent values and, 234–35
competence:
  aging and, 154–55
  family, 6–7, 23–24, 32, 54, 58, 146–52, 182